138TH OPEN CHAMPIONSHIP
Card of the Championship Course

Hole	Par	Yards	Hole	Par	Yards
1	4	354	10	4	456
2	4	428	11	3	175
3	4	489	12	4	451
4	3	166	13	4	410
5	4	474	14	4	448
6	3	231	15	3	206
7	5	538	16	4	455
8	4	454	17	5	559
9	4	449	18	4	461
Out	35	3,583	In	35	3,621
			Total	70	7,204

Aurum Press
7 Greenland Street, London NW1 0ND

Published 2009 by Aurum Press

Copyright © 2009 R&A Championships Limited

Statistics of The 138th Open Championship produced on a
Unisys Computer System

Course map courtesy of Dan Wardlaw, copyright © The Majors of Golf

Photograph on page 14 copyright © Brian Morgan

Assistance with records and research provided by Malcolm Booth,
Peter Lewis, Salvatore Johnson, and www.golfobserver.com

A CIP catalogue record for this book is available
from the British Library

ISBN-13: 978 1 84513 456 3

Designed and produced by Davis Design
Colour retouching by Luciano Retouching Services, Inc.
Printed in Great Britain by Purbrooks

WRITERS
Andy Farrell
Mike Aitken
John Hopkins
Lewine Mair
Alistair Tait

PHOTOGRAPHERS
Getty Images

David Cannon	Richard Martin-Roberts
Stuart Franklin	Mark Trowbridge
Richard Heathcote	*Golf Editors*
Harry How	
Ross Kinnaird	Scott Halleran
Warren Little	*Chief Editor*
Andrew Redington	

EDITOR
Bev Norwood

The Championship Committee

CHAIRMAN
Michael Brown

DEPUTY CHAIRMAN
Gavin Caldwell

COMMITTEE

Keith Andrews	Jeremy Monroe
David Bonsall	Richard Souter
JR Jones	Richard Stocks
Stuart Lloyd	Donald Turner
George MacGregor	Geoffrey Vero

CHIEF EXECUTIVE
Peter Dawson

DIRECTOR OF CHAMPIONSHIPS
David Hill

DIRECTOR OF RULES AND EQUIPMENT STANDARDS
David Rickman

Introduction

By Michael Brown

Chairman of the Championship Committee of The R&A

It was 15 years since the Championship had last been played at Turnberry in 1994, so its return for The 138th Open was keenly awaited. In the interval, the Ailsa course had been lengthened by around 250 yards, a number of bunkers had been added, and with the rough up after a good early spring it once again proved to be a demanding test.

The course was in outstanding condition from the outset and its presentation and set-up drew praise from the competitors. My thanks go to George Brown and his team for a really marvellous job — in George's case his third Open in charge at Turnberry — together with best wishes for his retirement.

The opening day was the most benign in recent memory and good scores duly followed. The final three days saw challenging sea breezes, occasionally strong and varying daily in direction, which showed Turnberry at its very best — and is there a finer view in golf?

Against this background a fascinating and thrilling Championship was played out with Tom Watson, always a favourite with the Scottish crowds, coming to the 72nd hole needing a par-4 to win his sixth Open 26 years after his fifth. Alas, it was just not to be, and Stewart Cink with a courageous 15-foot birdie putt on the home green tied his total and went on to become the worthy winner and The Champion Golfer for the first time in the ensuing playoff.

I must thank the Turnberry Championship Committee for all their assistance without which the successful staging of the Championship would not have been possible and our many volunteers for their help.

I hope you find the following pages an enjoyable reminder of a week which will live long in the memory of all who shared it.

Foreword

By Stewart Cink

There are so many words that could be used to describe how I feel about being The Open Champion, but I keep coming back to these: I'm filled with pride and honour.

The experience of that week at Turnberry is something I will never forget, to have outlasted everyone on that difficult golf course over the four days, then to have gone against none other than Tom Watson in the playoff. As I said at the time, I had mixed feelings about playing against Tom, because I had always watched him with such admiration.

For some reason I just believed all week that I was going to do something good. My swing felt great, I was hitting the ball solidly, and I felt so calm. I never felt nervous at all, not even in the last round in situations where in the past I would have been extremely nervous. I just felt calm all day. I was at peace about whatever happened because I was proud of how I had played. There's always somebody at a Major championship on Sunday who has that calm and peace about them, and I had it at Turnberry.

It can't get any more satisfying than this. All the work that I have put into my game has paid off. I have trusted myself that I would be able to transform my game, and I guess with The Claret Jug in my hands, it's now complete. The journey is not over, but I'm a believer now.

Golfing Heaven or Hell

By Andy Farrell

Weather can make all the difference, but George Brown says: "Turnberry is one of the fairest of golf courses. You get what you see."

There are days when there is not a breath of wind and the sun beats down from a cloudless sky and Turnberry is, indeed, the most scenic golf course in the world. Eight of the holes on the Ailsa course hug the shoreline where the Firth of Clyde meets the Irish Sea and the views take in the hills of the Isle of Arran, the Kintyre peninsula, and the prehistoric Ailsa Craig, rising 1,114 feet out of the water and fit only for birdlife. The first nine is played out towards the iconic symbol of the lighthouse, next to the ruins of Turnberry Castle, where Robert the Bruce, the Scottish king who banished the English at Bannockburn, was born in 1274. The second nine comes back towards the famous hotel, all red roof with sparklingly white walls, sitting on a ridge above, commanding all it surveys, land, sea and sky.

Preceding pages, scenes from around dawn at Turnberry on the first day of The 138th Open Championship.

"On a fresh day," wrote Pat Ward-Thomas, "with the sea tranquil and deepening in its blueness as the sun rises higher, or at evening when the mountains turn black in the fading light and the sky is livid with colour, Turnberry is incomparable." This is golfing heaven, even in winter, which can be surprisingly mild thanks to the Gulf Stream.

There are also days when the wind blows savagely — the tented village at the 1973 John Player Classic was swept out to sea — the rain comes in at right angles and visibility drops to the length of one of its formidable par 4s. This is golfing hell.

Of course, at Turnberry, these can be one and the same day.

Turnberry has a rich history and even if its association with The Open Championship is short — this is the fourth time The Claret Jug has been played for here — it has been every bit as dramatic as the weather. Turnberry is the most southerly, and most recent, of the three Ayrshire courses to host The Open. Prestwick Golf Club was the original home from 1860. Then came Royal Troon Golf Club in 1923, but Turnberry only arrived in 1977. Yet, that first Championship is one of the most famous ever,

The Turnberry Hotel opened in 1906, complete with a train station. The two golf courses opened three years earlier.

the so-called Duel in the Sun featuring Jack Nicklaus and Tom Watson. The temperatures were hot, the golf even hotter, as Watson edged Nicklaus by a single stroke after their epic 36-hole battle. Greg Norman, in 1986, and Nick Price, in 1994, were also crowned The Champion Golfer of the Year here.

It was the third Marquis of Ailsa, also the 14th Earl of Cassilis and owner of nearby Culzean Castle, who persuaded the Glasgow and South Western Railway, of which he was a director, to lease part of his land to build two golf courses and a luxury hotel. The Ailsa and the Arran courses were opened in 1903 and the hotel, complete with train station, in 1906. The place was a hit and only briefly disturbed during World War I when it was requisitioned as an air base.

Willie Fernie, an Open Champion who was the professional at Troon, laid out the original courses but over the years others made improvements. During World War II, when General Eisenhower had a base at Culzean Castle, the hotel was turned into a military hospital and again the courses were made into an airfield. However, this time the planes

were bigger and heavier and more numerous and the runways needed to be made of concrete. Both courses were ploughed up.

After the war, it was initially thought too expensive to re-construct the courses. But Frank Hole, chairman of British Transport Hotels Group, knew the hotel could not survive without its golf courses and eventually won compensation from the government. Thousands of tons of tarmac and hardcore were dug up, much of it used for coastal defences. Over 30,000 cubic yards of topsoil were brought in and spread over the courses, which were completely re-turfed. Signs of its wartime use remain in the shape of part of the runway flanking the inland holes — most useful when The Open arrived for parking and the tented village — while a memorial to the fallen overlooks the 12th green.

Philip Mackenzie Ross was the man who rebuilt the Ailsa course, and it re-opened in 1951. He did a fine job, according to Donald Steel, journalist turned architect: "There is no trickery or deceit. ... Mackenzie Ross struck the perfect balance between what is challenging and what is not." Some critics have noted how the Championship course, the Ailsa, a par 70, can yield dramatically low scoring and suggested it is a weakness. But, like any links, it is a question of taking what the conditions give you and being good enough to take advantage when there is the opportunity to do so.

"Any links, Birkdale or St Andrews or wherever, if they get calm, balmy days, they'll shoot 12 under and what's wrong with that?" said George Brown, the Turnberry estates manager. "But if the wind gets up, especially here, they will be nearer 84 than 64. Last year at The Amateur Championship, all four days the wind was from a different direction. That was wonderful, you had four different golf courses. You can't plan to have four 69s. You have to take what you can get, whether 84 or 64."

Brown arrived as head greenkeeper in 1986, just six months before The Open, and retired after his third Open in charge in 2009. "What I like about the course," he added, "I think Turnberry is one of the fairest of golf courses. You get what you see. I don't think it is any coincidence that in 1977 you had two of the best golfers of the time battling it out, in the mid-80s Greg Norman was one of the best golfers, and in the early to mid-90s Nick Price was one of the best. I think that says a lot for the course."

Turnberry's roll of honour is littered with champions. In 1921 Cecil Leitch won the Ladies British Amateur Championship but only after a fierce contest with Joyce Wethered, who would go on to be the dominant player of her day. Christy O'Connor Snr won the PGA Match Play in 1957 and Sandy Lyle the European Open in 1979. Sir Michael Bonallack won the first of his five Amateur titles at Turnberry in 1961, only having to play the 17th and 18th holes in the morning round of the final. The Walker Cup was played here in 1963 with the home team taking an early lead but then surrendering to the Americans on the second afternoon when ball after ball found Wilson's Burn on the 16th hole.

Karrie Webb, a former world number one, claimed the only Women's British Open to be played at Turnberry in 2002, while among winners of The Senior Open Championship here are Gary Player, Bob Charles and Tom Watson, in 2003, 26 years after the Duel in the Sun. "It is one of my favourite courses," Watson said. "You pretty much get what you deserve. There are not a lot of bad bounces. You pretty much can understand the golf course after playing a few rounds. It requires very good shot management, especially the ability to play in crosswinds. Do that, keep the ball out of the bunkers, and you can compete.

In the Words *of the* **Competitors...**

"You just can't fake it around this golf course. You have to hit good golf shots."

—Tiger Woods

"My whole links golfing life I've avoided the bunkers at all costs. Bunkers are like water hazards on a links golf course."

—Padraig Harrington

"It's a beautiful course in good condition and a very scenic place, and it's going to be good fun to play it."

—Henrik Stenson

"It's a tough golf course, a good golf course. And with a 10 or 15 mile-an-hour wind, I think the golf course is going to play very tough."

—Ian Poulter

"It's got some brilliant golf holes. I think 16 is one of my favourite holes in the world."

—Paul Casey

"Turnberry, from a player standpoint, has it all. You stay in the hotel, you walk down the hill, you get on the driving range, you never put a key in the ignition of your car."

—Greg Norman

"Naturally, winning The Open at Turnberry is one of the championships I most cherish," Watson added. "To beat Jack Nicklaus that year and for us to play as well as we did was special."

Watson won the first of his five Open titles on his debut in 1975 at Carnoustie. Until he won the Masters in 1977, holding off Nicklaus in the final round, he had a reputation for not finishing the job off in Majors. Nicklaus was a 14-Major winner and 10 years Watson's senior. After two rounds they shared second place, one behind Roger Maltbie, and played together in the third round. Both scored rounds of 65 and now they were three ahead of Ben Crenshaw. Nicklaus was soon three ahead, but Watson levelled at the eighth. On the ninth the gallery had become so large and uncontrollable that the players halted while order was restored. Nicklaus went ahead again and was two in front with six to play.

Yet again Watson responded and holed a big putt from the fringe at the 15th for a birdie which Nicklaus could not match. On the 16th tee Watson said to his opponent: "This is what it's all about, isn't it?" Nicklaus replied: "You bet it is." Watson found the 17th green in two and got his birdie-4, but Nicklaus could not get up and down so slipped one back. At the last, Nicklaus' drive found the edge of a gorse bush, but Watson was in prime position and striped a 7-iron to two feet. Nicklaus slashed out of the bush and got the ball onto the green but

Jack Nicklaus and Tom Watson at the end of their 1977 duel.

looked doomed. Until he holed the putt from over 35 feet, that is. Watson always assumed Nicklaus would find a way to make his 3. He was not shaken and holed out for his own 3 and the victory. "I'm tired of giving it my best shot and coming up short," Nicklaus told his young conqueror as they left the green arm-in-arm.

Watson set records for the lowest final round by a Champion, another 65, the lowest score for the last 36 holes of 130, and the lowest total of 268. Both he and Nicklaus (269) smashed the old record of 276 set by Arnold Palmer. Mark Hayes also set an Open record for the lowest round with 63 in the second round, two lower than the old mark first set by Henry Cotton. But despite the accusation that the baked-out course, with the thinnest of rough, was defenceless, Hubert Green, the reigning US Open champion, was the only other player to beat par at one under, 11 behind Watson. "I won the tournament I was playing in," Green said. "They were playing in something else."

Nine years later conditions were very different. The rough was thick, and that was fine in practice when the air was still, but on the Thursday the wind picked up and the rain was of the sideways variety. Nevertheless, in the second round, Norman matched Hayes' 63. The Australian had a putt at the last for a 61 but three-putted for his third bogey of the round, which otherwise contained an eagle, eight birdies and six pars. It was the year Norman

Round Turnberry

No 1 Ailsa Craig • 354 yards Par 4
A short par 4 to open with and possibly driveable, although new bunkers have changed the risk-reward ratio. A slight dogleg to the right, the hole features four bunkers down the left — with new ones at 280 and 300 yards — and one on the right, plus four around the green itself.

No 2 Mak Siccar • 428 yards Par 4
Another par 4 turning to the left but has been left virtually unchanged. The greenside bunker on the left has been cut closer to the green, and a partner bunker guards the entrance on the right. A sharp fall-away on the left of the green needs to be avoided.

No 3 Blaw Wearie • 489 yards Par 4
It runs parallel to the previous two holes. A new back tee has been built, two bunkers added at 260 and 300 yards on the left of the fairway, and a bunker to the left of the green turned into a grassy hollow. Two bunkers guard the right side of the green.

No 4 Woe-Be-Tide • 166 yards Par 3
The first short hole and the first of eight to run along the coast. A classic par 3 played to an elevated green with a big bunker short right to be carried. The greens falls away front and left, while bushes top a bank on the right.

No 5 Fin Me Oot • 474 yards Par 4
A strong par 4 sweeping round to the left. An old back tee has been brought back into play, lengthening the hole by 33 yards. There are two fairway bunkers on the left and two new ones on the right at 290 and 320 yards. Bunkers in front of the green foreshorten the approach shot.

No 6 Tappie Toorie • 231 yards Par 3
Another difficult par 3 played to a raised green. There is a big bunker front right and three bunkers on the left. Anything short rolls back down the slope.

No 7 Roon the Ben • 538 yards Par 5
The first of only two long holes is, as the name suggests, a big dogleg round a hill to the left. The biggest change here is the crater on the left just short of the green which has been extended further into the fairway, forcing any lay-up shot or a long approach to be positioned with more accuracy.

No 8 Goat Fell • 454 yards Par 4
Another strong par 4 with a new tee to the right of the old one extending the hole and straightening it out. This brings into play the old bunker on the right of the fairway and the two new ones beyond it at 300 and 325 yards. The raised green has a significant ridge running across it.

No 9 Bruce's Castle • 449 yards Par 4
No change at one of the course's most famous holes. The Championship tee is out on a rocky outcrop, while the fairway is a hogsback, but there are no bunkers. The ruins of Turnberry Castle, where Robert the Bruce was born, are on the left.

No 10 Dinna Fouter • 456 yards Par 4
A dramatic new tee has been positioned right under the famous lighthouse and forces a carry across the beach. The fairway has been moved closer to the coast with three new bunkers added on the right. Now a great driving hole.

No 11 Maidens • 175 yards Par 3
Named after the nearby town, a good par 3 which is virtually unchanged. Two bunkers guard the entrance to the green, left and right, so the most difficult hole locations are at the front of the putting surface.

No 12 Monument • 451 yards Par 4
The course now turns inland again with a straight par 4. To the three bunkers on the left has been added another on the right at 320 yards. The war memorial stands tall on the bank to the right of the green.

No 13 Tickly Tap • 410 yards Par 4
A dogleg to the right with the corner guarded by a newly created ridge, while a new bunker on the left has been added to make the drive more testing. The green is raised, angled to the left but not guarded by any bunkers.

No 14 Risk-an-Hope • 448 yards Par 4
Now a good driving hole with two bunkers out on the right of the fairway and humps and hollows created on the left. In addition, a new tee to the left of the original is used to give a better view of the fairway. Three bunkers guard the green, which falls away back right.

No 15 Ca' Canny • 206 yards Par 3
Yet another strong par 3 and one that did not require any changes for this year's Open. Three bunkers guard the left side of the green, while anything right will drop down the gully and prove a testing up-and-down.

No 16 Wee Burn • 455 yards Par 4
A terrific new hole now that the fairway has been moved to the left, making it a dogleg. The old bunker on the left is now on the right of the fairway with a new bunker on the left. Then the approach, with anything from a mid to a short iron depending on the wind, needs to carry Wilson's Burn which runs in front and to the right of the green.

No 17 Lang Whang • 559 yards Par 5
A new back tee has been added, where the old 16th fairway was, extending the hole by 61 yards. Played through a valley to an elevated green with new bunkers added to make the approach more tricky. A long, thin green down which Nick Price holed for eagle in 1994.

No 18 Duel in the Sun • 461 yards Par 4
Named after the famous 1977 Open, the hole makes for a sharp dogleg to the left, with the corner now guarded by three bunkers, while the great gorse bushes remain on the right. The approach to the green has been enhanced with a new bunker on each side of the fairway, while the green is angled slightly to the left.

Greg Norman won here in 1986 for his first Major.

In 1994, Nick Price won after holing from 50 feet on 17 for eagle.

led all four Major championships on the Saturday evening, but he only claimed The Open, closing with 69 to win by five strokes from Gordon J Brand. The winning score was level-par.

But in 1994 the sunshine was back, and Price matched Watson's 12-under aggregate after four rounds in the 60s. The climax was extraordinary with Price holing a curling 50-footer down the length of the 17th green for an eagle. Jesper Parnevik, the Swede with an aversion to looking at leaderboards, thought he needed to birdie the last to win but missed the green and took a bogey. Price made his par and claimed The Claret Jug that had eluded him earlier in his career. A month later he won his third Major title at the US PGA Championship and was briefly the world's best player.

It took 15 years for The Open to return, not due to the quality of the golf course but because there were difficulties with traffic that needed to be resolved on the road down from Ayr.

The delay allowed time for some changes to be made to the Ailsa course. Chief among them were a new tee at the 10th, under the nose of the lighthouse, forcing a carry across the shoreline and making a companion for the dramatic Championship tee at the ninth on its own rocky outcrop. In addition, the fairway at the 16th was moved to the left, making the hole a dogleg and bringing Wilson's Burn in front of the green more into play. This also allowed the tee at the par-5 17th to be moved back. Other tees also went back, as the course was extended to 7,204 yards, while the number of fairway bunkers increased from 66 to 87. "They are quite penal, the players won't like them," said Brown. "They're going to put more of an emphasis on accuracy."

Off the course, too, there have been changes at Turnberry with the hotel and courses bought for £55 million in 2008 by Leisurecorp, an investment company from the UAE which was behind the European Tour's Race to Dubai. Over the winter the hotel was gutted and renovated in time to receive its distinguished visitors for The Open.

Included among them, Tiger Woods and Padraig Harrington had never played here in competition before. A new era was beginning.

Exempt Competitors

Name, Country	Category
Robert Allenby, Australia	1, 5, 15
Stephen Ames, Canada	1, 5
Stuart Appleby, Australia	15
Briny Baird, USA	15
Mark Brown, New Zealand	21
Angel Cabrera, Argentina	5, 11, 12
Mark Calcavecchia, USA	3
Chad Campbell, USA	5, 15, 19
Michael Campbell, New Zealand	11
Paul Casey, England	1, 5, 6, 7, 19
KJ Choi, South Korea	5, 15
Stewart Cink, USA	5, 15, 19
Tim Clark, South Africa	5, 15
Darren Clarke, Northern Ireland	6
Ben Crane**, USA	5
Ben Curtis, USA	1, 3, 4, 5, 15, 19
John Daly, USA	3
Luke Donald, England	5
Nick Dougherty, England	9
Ken Duke, USA	15
David Duval, USA	3, 4
Johan Edfors, Sweden	9
Ernie Els, South Africa	1, 3, 4, 5, 15
Sir Nick Faldo, England	3
Gonzalo Fernandez-Castano, Spain	5
Richard Finch, England	6
Ross Fisher, England	5, 6
Jim Furyk, USA	1, 5, 15, 19
Sergio Garcia, Spain	5, 6, 14, 15, 19
Brian Gay, USA	16
Lucas Glover, USA	11
Mathew Goggin**, Australia	5
Retief Goosen, South Africa	5, 6
Paul Goydos, USA	17
Richard Green, Australia	6
Stephan Gross*, Germany	30
Todd Hamilton, USA	3, 4
Anders Hansen, Denmark	7
Soren Hansen, Denmark	6, 19
Peter Hanson, Sweden	6
Padraig Harrington, Republic of Ireland	1, 3, 4, 5, 6, 13, 19
Peter Hedblom, Sweden	6
Charley Hoffman, USA	16
JB Holmes, USA	19
Charles Howell III, USA	16
David Howell, England	1
Yuta Ikeda, Japan	26
Ryuji Imada, Japan	15
Ryo Ishikawa, Japan	25
Thongchai Jaidee, Thailand	8
Miguel Angel Jimenez, Spain	5, 6, 7, 19
Dustin Johnson, USA	5
Zach Johnson, USA	5, 12
Martin Kaymer, Germany	5, 6
Anthony Kim, USA	1, 5, 15, 19
James Kingston, South Africa	6
Soren Kjeldsen, Denmark	5, 6
Tomohiro Kondo, Japan	25
Kenichi Kuboya, Japan	25
Pablo Larrazabal, Spain	6
Paul Lawrie, Scotland	3, 4
Tom Lehman, USA	3
Justin Leonard, USA	3, 5, 15, 19
Thomas Levet**, France	5
Sandy Lyle, Scotland	3
Hunter Mahan, USA	5, 15, 19
Matteo Manassero*, Italy	28
Steve Marino**, USA	5
Prayad Marksaeng, Thailand	24
Billy Mayfair, USA	15
Graeme McDowell, Northern Ireland	5, 6, 19
Paul McGinley, Republic of Ireland	6
Damien McGrane, Republic of Ireland	6
Rory McIlroy, Northern Ireland	5
Bryce Molder, USA	17
Francesco Molinari, Italy	6
Colin Montgomerie, Scotland	6
Greg Norman, Australia	1, 3
Koumei Oda, Japan	26
Geoff Ogilvy, Australia	5, 11
Sean O'Hair, USA	5
Mark O'Meara, USA	3
Louis Oosthuizen, South Africa	8
Rod Pampling**, Australia	5
Kenny Perry, USA	5, 15, 19
Carl Pettersson, Sweden	15
Ian Poulter, England	1, 5, 6, 19
Alvaro Quiros, Spain	5, 6
Robert Rock, England	8
Andres Romero, Argentina	15
Justin Rose, England	5, 19
Rory Sabbatini, South Africa	5
Charl Schwartzel, South Africa	6
Adam Scott, Australia	5
John Senden**, Australia	5
Vijay Singh, Fiji	5, 13, 15
David Smail, New Zealand	25

Name, Country	Category	Name, Country	Category
Brandt Snedeker, USA	18	Bubba Watson, USA	15
Henrik Stenson, Sweden	1, 5, 6, 19	Tom Watson, USA	3
Richard Sterne, South Africa	22	Boo Weekley, USA	19
Steve Stricker, USA	1, 5, 15, 19	Mike Weir, Canada	5, 15
Kevin Sutherland, USA	15	Lee Westwood, England	5, 6, 19
David Toms, USA	5	Oliver Wilson, England	5, 6, 19
DJ Trahan, USA	15	Chris Wood, England	1
Bruce Vaughan, USA	27	Tiger Woods, USA	3, 4, 5, 11, 12, 13
Camilo Villegas, Colombia	5, 15	Azuma Yano, Japan	24
Anthony Wall, England	6		
Nick Watney, USA	5		

* Denotes amateurs   **Denotes reserves

Key to Exemptions from Regional, Local Final and International Final Qualifying

Exemptions for 2009 were granted to the following:

(1) First 10 and anyone tying for 10th place in the 2008 Open Championship at Royal Birkdale.

(2) Past Open Champions born between 17 July 1943 - 19 July 1948.

(3) Past Open Champions aged 60 or under on 19 July 2009.

(4) The Open Champions for 1999-2008.

(5) The first 50 players on the Official World Golf Ranking for Week 21, 2009, intended publication date Monday 25 May 2009.

(6) First 30 in the final European Tour Order of Merit for 2008.

(7) The BMW PGA Championship winners for 2007-2009.

(8) First 3 and anyone tying for 3rd place, not otherwise exempt, in the top 20 of the Race to Dubai for 2009 on completion of the 2009 BMW PGA Championship.

(9) First 2 European Tour members and any European Tour members tying for 2nd place, not otherwise exempt, in a cumulative money list taken from all official PGA European Tour events from the Official World Golf Ranking for Week 19 up to and including the BMW International and including The US Open.

(10) The leading player, not otherwise exempt, in the first 5 and ties of each of the 2009 Open de France ALSTOM and the 2009 Barclays Scottish Open. Ties will be decided by the better final round score and, if still tied, by the better third round score and then by the better second round score. If still tied, a hole by hole card playoff will take place starting at the 18th hole of the final round.

(11) The US Open Champions for 2005-2009.

(12) The US Masters Champions for 2005-2009.

(13) The US PGA Champions for 2004-2008.

(14) The PLAYERS Champions for 2007-2009.

(15) The leading 30 qualifiers for the 2008 TOUR CHAMPIONSHIP.

(16) First 3 and anyone tying for 3rd place, not exempt having applied (5) above, in the top 20 of the PGA TOUR FedExCup Points List for 2009 on completion of the HP Byron Nelson Championship.

(17) First 2 US PGA TOUR members and any US PGA TOUR members tying for 2nd place, not exempt, in a cumulative money list taken from the US PGA TOUR PLAYERS Championship and the five US PGA TOUR events leading up to and including the 2009 AT&T National.

(18) The leading player, not exempt having applied (17) above, in the first 5 and ties of each of the 2009 AT&T National and the 2009 John Deere Classic. Ties will be decided by the better final round score and, if still tied, by the better third round score and then by the better second round score. If still tied, a hole by hole card playoff will take place starting at the 18th hole of the final round.

(19) Playing members of the 2008 Ryder Cup teams.

(20) First and anyone tying for 1st place on the Order of Merit of the Asian Tour for 2008.

(21) First and anyone tying for 1st place on the Order of Merit of the Tour of Australasia for 2008.

(22) First and anyone tying for 1st place on the Order of Merit of the Southern Africa PGA Sunshine Tour for 2008.

(23) The Japan Open Champion for 2008.

(24) First 2 and anyone tying for 2nd place, not exempt, on the Official Money List of the Japan Golf Tour for 2008.

(25) The leading 4 players, not exempt, in the 2009 Mizuno Open Yomiuri Classic. Ties will be decided by the better final round score and, if still tied, by the better third round score and then by the better second round score. If still tied, a hole by hole card playoff will take place starting at the 18th hole of the final round.

(26) First 2 and anyone tying for 2nd place, not exempt having applied (25) above, in a cumulative money list taken from all official 2009 Japan Golf Tour events up to and including the 2009 Mizuno Open Yomiuri Classic.

(27) The Senior Open Champion for 2008.

(28) The Amateur Champion for 2009.

(29) The US Amateur Champion for 2008.

(30) The European Amateur Champion for 2008. *(28) to (30) are only applicable if the entrant concerned is still an amateur on 16 July 2009.*

Local Final Qualifying
6 & 7 July

Glasgow Gailes Links
Thomas Aiken, South Africa	69 67	136
Peter Baker, England	69 69	138
Elliot Saltman, Scotland	67 72	139
David Higgins, Rep. of Ireland	70 69	139

Kilmarnock (Barassie)
Markus Brier, Austria	64 66	130
Lloyd Saltman, Scotland	66 70	136
Daniel Gaunt, Australia	69 67	136
Peter Ellebye, Denmark	68 68	136

Western Gailes
Fredrik Andersson Hed, Sweden	70 67	137
Steve Surry, England	72 66	138
Thomas Haylock, England	73 67	140
Daniel Wardrop, England	72 68	140

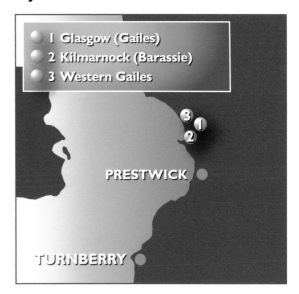

1 Glasgow (Gailes)
2 Kilmarnock (Barassie)
3 Western Gailes

PRESTWICK

TURNBERRY

The Starting Field

"G. In the event of an exempt player withdrawing from the Championship or further places becoming available in the starting field after the close of entries, these places will be allocated in the ranking order of entrants from OWGR (Official World Golf Ranking) at the time that intimation of withdrawal is received or further places are made available by the Championship Committee. Any withdrawals following issue of OWGR Week 27 will be taken in ranking order from OWGR Week 27."

Mathew Goggin, Australia, replaced Trevor Immelman, South Africa
Ben Crane, USA, replaced Phil Mickelson, USA
Steve Marino, USA, replaced Shingo Katayama, Japan
John Senden, Australia, replaced Jeev Milkha Singh, India

Elliot Saltman

Daniel Gaunt

David Higgins

Peter Baker

International Final Qualifying

ASIA **31 March & 1 April**

Sentosa   *Singapore*

Gaganjeet Bhullar, India	69	67	136
Wen-chong Liang, China	72	66	138
Terry Pilkadaris, Australia	67	72	139
Tim Stewart[(P)], Australia	70	70	140

[(P)] Qualified after playoff

Gaganjeet Bhullar

AMERICA **25 May**

Gleneagles   *Plano, Texas*

Matt Kuchar, USA	63	66	129
Jeff Overton, USA	64	67	131
Davis Love III, USA	67	65	132
Richard S Johnson, Sweden	65	67	132
James Driscoll, USA	67	65	132
Tim Wilkinson*, New Zealand	65	67	132
Fredrik Jacobson, Sweden	68	64	132
Martin Laird, Scotland	67	65	132

*Withdrew

Matt Kuchar

AUSTRALASIA **10 February**

Kingston Heath   *Melbourne, Australia*

Josh Geary, New Zealand	70	70	140
Timothy Wood, Australia	71	69	140
Michael Wright, Australia	69	72	141

Timothy Wood

Turnberry

EUROPE   8 June

Sunningdale   *Berkshire, England*

Rafa Echenique, Argentina	66	64	130
Graeme Storm, England	62	68	130
David Drysdale, Scotland	65	66	131
Gary Orr, Scotland	68	63	131
Branden Grace, South Africa	65	66	131
Raphael Jacquelin, France	64	68	132
Paul Broadhurst, England	65	67	132
Rhys Davies, Wales	65	67	132
Oliver Fisher[P], England	66	67	133
Richard Ramsay[P], Scotland	65	68	133

[P]Qualified after playoff

Rafa Echenique

AFRICA   3 & 4 February

Royal Durban   *Durban, South Africa*

Marc Cayeux, Zimbabwe	69	68	137
Jaco Ahlers, South Africa	73	65	138
Jeremy Kavanagh, England	67	71	138

Marc Cayeux

One of Those Glorious Days

By Andy Farrell

There was no finer place to be than Turnberry, especially for Tom Watson and, later, Miguel Angel Jimenez.

If this was supposed to be a new era for The Open Championship at Turnberry, then nobody told Tom Watson. A quick glance at the leaderboard for much of the first round reminded one of the 1970s and 1980s. The Watson of old dominated The Open back then, and now, at 59, Watson was dominating the challenge for The Claret Jug once again. If the fact that his name, such a welcome surprise among the contenders, was ultimately eclipsed at the top of the leaderboard by the end of the day was some kind of omen for the eventual climax on Sunday night, this was no time to be heeding the warning.

For this was about as joyful as opening to an Open as could be imagined. It was one of those glorious days at Turnberry, sunny and calm, when

---

In the evening Miguel Angel Jimenez was left standing on 64 with the lead by one stroke over three others.

there is no finer place to be. "I love my office," Watson said on the first tee of his final practice round, and after opening with a 65, he continued: "There was something slightly spiritual about today. I feel inspired playing here again."

No one in the first half of the draw, which included world number one Tiger Woods and Greg Norman, who at the age of 53 himself made a romantic challenge at the 2008 Open, could match Watson, so that grand old name sat above all others on the leaderboard for most of the afternoon. Finally, Ben Curtis, the 2003 Champion, joined Watson on 65, as Kenichi Kuboya did as dusk descended, but it was not until shortly before 7pm that Miguel Angel Jimenez, after birdies at the final two holes, posted the day's best score of 64, six under-par.

The late golf writer Dai Davies, of the *Birmingham Post* and *The Guardian*, had a technique for circumventing those who with no regard for deadlines or dinner reservations threatened to spoil a well-crafted and otherwise complete article. He would preface it with the words: "If, for one moment, you put to one side the achievements of Joe Bloggs, the round of the day came from...." Jimenez is too generous

1

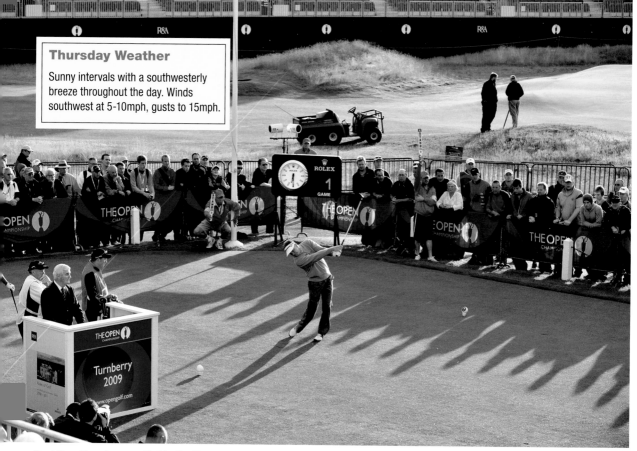

Paul Broadhurst was called to the first tee at 6.30am to start The 138th Open Championship.

a soul not to recognise that his best ever round at The Open, by three strokes, was not the main story of the day. "What a legend," he said of the man he demoted into second place. "He was a legend before, he was a legend today, and he will be a legend tomorrow. We have to feel proud to play with him."

A 65 was a fitting number for Watson. It was the fourth time he had returned the score in his fourth Open here. He did so in the second round in 1994, when aged merely 44 he had another run at a sixth Open title but was let down by his putting, and, of course, in the third and fourth rounds in 1977 when he defeated Jack Nicklaus by a single stroke in what will forever be known as the Duel in the Sun.

It is an interesting insight into great champions that Nicklaus says he cannot remember a single shot of that final round, while Watson remembers every one. "Whenever you play a golf course where you have had success, where you have hit quality shots, that helps you," Watson said. "I am playing off the memories of '77." Watson had also played in two Senior Open Championships at Turnberry, winning in 2003. "This is my sixth Championship here and you do get to know the course. Experience helps. There are certain shots out here that the kids are unfamiliar with, that people who haven't played here before are unfamiliar with." With The Open returning to Turnberry for the first time since 1994, among the newcomers were Woods and double defending Champion Padraig Harrington.

Helped by a hip replacement the previous October that enabled him to return to the Champions Tour during 2009, Watson showed all his old expertise in tacking his way around a links. He drove the ball superbly, eagerly marched up the fairways, hit his irons as crisply as ever, and gave anyone

First Round Leaders

HOLE	1	2	3	4	5	6	7	8	9	10	11	12	13	14	15	16	17	18	
PAR	4	4	4	3	4	3	5	4	4	4	3	4	4	4	3	4	5	4	TOTAL
Miguel Angel Jimenez	4	(3)	4	3	4	(2)	(4)	4	(3)	4	3	4	4	4	3	4	(4)	(3)	64
Tom Watson	(3)	4	(3)	3	4	3	5	4	4	(3)	3	(3)	4	4	3	4	(4)	4	65
Ben Curtis	4	4	4	[4]	(3)	3	(3)	4	4	[5]	3	4	(3)	(3)	3	(3)	(4)	4	65
Kenichi Kuboya	4	4	4	[4]	[5]	3	(4)	(3)	4	4	3	4	(3)	[5]	(2)	(3)	(3)	(3)	65
John Senden	4	4	4	3	4	3	5	4	4	4	3	4	(3)	(3)	(2)	4	(4)	4	66
Steve Stricker	4	(3)	4	3	4	3	5	(3)	[5]	[5]	(2)	(3)	4	4	3	4	(4)	(3)	66
Camilo Villegas	[5]	4	4	(2)	4	3	5	4	4	4	3	4	4	(3)	3	(3)	(4)	(3)	66
Stewart Cink	4	4	4	(2)	4	(2)	5	(3)	4	(3)	[4]	4	(3)	4	3	4	(4)	[5]	66
Mathew Goggin	[5]	(3)	4	(2)	4	3	(4)	(3)	4	4	3	4	[5]	4	3	4	(4)	(3)	66

Tom Watson responded to the applause after his 65, the same score as for his third and fourth rounds 32 years ago.

Tom Watson's playing partners Sergio Garcia (above) and Matteo Manassero (far right) were a combined 45 years of age to Watson's 59.

Kenichi Kuboya (right) birdied the last four holes for 65.

The 2003 Champion, Ben Curtis, was near the top again, on 65.

who had missed his supremacy of links golf — he won five Opens in nine years between 1975 and 1983 — a masterful lesson in how golf can be art rather than being reduced to the science of modern engineering.

Neither of his playing partners was born when Watson and Nicklaus duelled here 32 years earlier. Sergio Garcia, 29, said: "He flushed it today. The quality of his ball-striking was awesome. If he plays the way he played today he can beat Tiger Woods and everyone else."

Matteo Manassero, the 16-year-old Italian who a month earlier had become the youngest ever winner of The Amateur Championship, was simply open-mouthed at the wonder of it all. "It was a great experience, it was fantastic," he said. "Tom was unbelievable and Sergio was great, too." Garcia had a 70, level-par, and Manassero a 71.

The threesome went off at 7.58am. "Sometimes, when you get to my age, you don't know how you are going to wake up. The golf swing might be there, it might not," Watson said. It was there. At the first he hit a 9-iron to eight feet and holed the putt for a birdie. He missed from 12 feet at the next but made one from 20 feet at the third to go two under. "She was defenceless today," Watson said of the course. "It gave you some opportunities with the lack of wind. After the practice rounds I felt good about the way I was hitting the ball and the first few holes were a nice continuation of that. I hit a lot of quality shots."

Excerpts FROM THE Press

"The history of The Open Championship is full of memorable moments and the 138th edition was not long in producing another. At the age of 59, Tom Watson's five-under-par 65 at Turnberry was just such an event, and those who witnessed it will thank their lucky stars for having done so."

—Graham Spiers, *The Times*

"Winning The Amateur Championship earned 16-year-old Italian Matteo Manassero the chance to play with his idol. No, not five-time Open Champion Tom Watson but Sergio Garcia. Bet that made El Nino feel old."

—Nick Hoult, *The Daily Telegraph*

"Tiger Woods spoke earlier this week about how Turnberry rewards good golf. He must now also accept that it does not always punish bad golf. Woods somehow emerged from an uninspired opening round still in contention."

—Alan Pattullo, *The Scotsman*

"The best golfers in the world will never have an easier day on an Open golf course."

—Jock MacVicar, *Daily Express*

"When Ben Curtis won The Open on his first try, he seemed one of the most unlikely Major champions in golf history. Beyond family and friends, no one had ever heard of the guy. It's different now. … Curtis has proven a worthy Champion."

—Paul Newberry, *The Associated Press*

Mathew Goggin scored a 66 with a birdie at the last.

Camilo Villegas finished on 66, closing with three birdies.

He did not drop a stroke to par all day. He went to the turn in 33 and then hit a 6-iron to 12 feet at the 10th and holed from eight feet at the 12th for birdies. He got up and down from a bunker at the 14th and then made two good putts at the last two holes. He holed from eight feet for his fifth birdie at the 17th and, after hitting in a fine 7-iron at the last and racing his birdie attempt, he made the one back from six feet for a par. "I wanted to finish strongly," he said. "The reason I am still out here is that I love to compete and to hit a shot when it really counts, like the approach at the last."

Watson revealed that Barbara Nicklaus, Jack's

Steve Stricker's 66 included bogeys on the ninth and 10th holes.

Stewart Cink returned a 66, including a birdie here on 10.

Surprise, Surprise
Why Calcavecchia Loves The Open

There was some surprise when Mark Calcavecchia won The Open at Royal Troon in 1989 on only his third attempt, but there should not have been. Calcavecchia, 29, was a good young player, a putter who knew no fear, and a crisp iron player.

There was some surprise when a 67 by Calcavecchia, 49, put him among the leaders after the first round this year, but, again, there should not have been. It was a day when age mattered far less than skill. The lead was held by Miguel Angel Jimenez, who was 45 and was one stroke ahead of Tom Watson, who was 59.

Despite a dodgy back and an unathletic build, Calcavecchia had won the 2005 Canadian Open when he was 45, and the PODS Championship in 2007 when he was 47. So he could still play.

Perhaps more important was that he could still play links golf. It didn't matter that he was in the first group off, starting at 6.30am, because that meant that he, a man who plays golf as if he has a train to catch, Michael Campbell and Paul Broadhurst moved around the course at their own speed. "We had the place to ourselves. On the 15th tee I'm looking around and the group behind us were on the 11th green and I'm like, well, thank goodness we're in front of them not behind them."

It was a sight to see Calcavecchia in his 23rd consecutive Open battling into what wind there was, his wife Brenda on his bag alongside him. Yet far from wishing he was back home, he loved it. He gets The Open as Tom Watson does and Jack Nicklaus used to and that is why he has played in every one since starting at Muirfield in 1987.

"I've always told people who ask what's your favourite place to play or your favourite tournament, the same answer: the British Open. The Open. It's my favourite. I am going to play in it until I am 60. I love it."

Proving the old adage that if you like something you are probably good at it, Calcavecchia had birdies on the second, seventh, 11th and 17th holes and dropped a stroke on the third. He made it seem easy.

—**John Hopkins**

First Round Scores	
Players Under Par	50
Players At Par	17
Players Over Par	89

wife, had sent him a good luck text on Wednesday and he had replied that it was not the same without Jack playing in the tournament. This prompted a rather impertinent question from a much younger member of the media that he wasn't sure what was more impressive, "your score or that someone of your age can actually send a text." Watson took it in good part, but added: "Don't ask me to Twitter. I don't tweet."

But in this modern world lots do, including inevitably Ian Poulter, who today was more notable for his outfit of Union Jack cardigan and tartan trousers than his score (75), and veteran American journalist Dan Jenkins, attending his 201st Major championship, who on another sartorial issue tweeted: "John Daly, the trailer park called after seeing your pants. They want their shower curtains back." Another to get into the craze is Stewart Cink, who the previous week had been revealing details of his family golfing holiday in Ireland and teaching his son to drive a right-hand drive manual car in the car park at Doonbeg. Since signing onto Twitter a few months earlier Cink had collected over half a million followers.

Tennis stars Chris Evert (left, wife of Greg Norman) and Ana Ivanovic (girlfriend of Adam Scott) were prominent in the crowds.

The fashions of Ian Poulter (left) and John Daly (and girlfriend Anna Cladakis) drew as much comment as their play.

"Adam Scott's girlfriend, tennis star Ana Ivanovic, looked like she was having a ball as she patrolled the fairways to follow the Australian's progress to level-par 70."

—Mike Dickson, *Daily Mail*

"Sadly for home hopes there was not a single Briton, far less a Scot, in the top 20, and Miguel Angel Jimenez was the sole European on the leaderboard."

—Douglas Lowe, *The Herald*

"Patriotic English showman Ian Poulter caught the eye at Turnberry wearing a Union Jack top on the links. But the Ryder Cup ace, who came second in The Open last year, carded a disappointing 75 to end up five over."

—James Nursey, *Daily Mirror*

"Miguel Angel Jimenez had a message for Seve Ballesteros after taking the first-round lead in The Open. Ballesteros held The Claret Jug aloft three times, but is now recovering from four operations to remove a brain tumour. 'Seve's meant a lot for the Tour, for lots of people,' said Jimenez after a six-under 64."

—Mark Garrod, *Press Association*

"The reaction was as loud as his trousers when John Daly almost holed his second shot for an albatross on the 538-yard par-5 seventh. Daly chased an iron up on the green and it seemed certain to drop before horseshoeing the cup."

—James Corrigan, *The Independent*

Jim Furyk posted a 67 with birdies on the 14th and 17th.

Mark O'Meara's 67 matched his Open low score.

"The best thing for me is that now I've got people who are getting a glimpse of Stewart Cink the person and not just what they see on television," he explained. "It's a way for me to build a fan base. I love the veil being lifted because I've struggled behind the veil for many years."

The trip to Ireland had a serious side, as the only other time he had undertaken such preparation for The Open he had finished tied for sixth at Carnoustie in 2007, the only time he had made the cut in his previous four appearances. Playing an hour and a half behind Watson, Cink came in with a 66, which included 2s at both the fourth and the sixth holes as well as a second bogey of the day at the 18th. No one managed fewer than his 26 putts, a welcome boost for his confidence after ditching the long putter a couple of months earlier.

But the talk was of Watson. "I am not surprised to see him up there," Cink said. "Tom Watson is one of the best ball-strikers of all time and he knows his way around here. It reminds me of a practice round I played with him at the Masters this year when it was blowing about 30mph and it was cold.

Paul Casey went out in 31 for his 68.

Graeme McDowell, on 68, was content not to lead this time.

I didn't even want to be out there, but I don't think he missed a shot. He hit every tee shot down the fairway and every iron shot at the flag. It was very impressive for a guy of that age on a tough course like Augusta National. He must have his ball-striking in the same place he had then."

Watson admitted that he could not compete at Augusta any more with all the changes they had made, but on a British seaside links it was a different story.

He was not the only former Champion enjoying a good day. Mark O'Meara, the 1998 Champion, had a 67, matching his lowest score in the Championship, as did Mark Calcavecchia (1989), while Daly (1995) had a 68 after hitting the flag with his second at the seventh and having just a tap-in for an eagle.

It was 20 years since Calcavecchia won at Royal Troon. Despite a back spasm during the final day of the John Deere Classic the previous Sunday while having to play 36 holes — his remedy was a cocktail of painkillers and beer — the 49-year-old was up bright and early to play in the first group of the day at 6.30am. "The weather was perfect and I get up early no matter what country I'm in," he said. "I hate to say Turnberry was easy, because it's a really hard course, but if you are going to shoot a good score out there, today was the day to do it." Only a bogey at the third spoilt his card.

John Senden, an Australian based in Dallas who was the seventh

All eyes — and cameras — were on the 9.09am group from the first tee.

Lee Westwood started with three birdies.

Tiger Woods was continually offline.

reserve and only got into the Championship on the Tuesday, parred his first 12 holes and then collected four birdies in the last six. He was the first to return a 66, where he was joined by Steve Stricker, the John Deere Classic winner, Camilo Villegas, who birdied the last three holes, Cink, and Mathew Goggin, another US-based Australian.

But on this opening morning all eyes had started off watching the 9.09am group which featured Woods, Lee Westwood, and Ryo Ishikawa, the 17-year-old Japanese sensation. A great cavalcade of officials, photographers, and reporters went off with them, and if Westwood felt any lack of attention alongside two players whose every move is monitored in minute detail, then three birdies at the first three holes quickly put that right. At the short fourth he put his tee shot to four feet but missed the putt for a fourth birdie in a row. After that the Englishman, who was in form at the French and Scottish Opens the previous two weeks, was steady rather than spectacular, but a double-bogey at the 16th was a costly mistake.

Both he and Tiger were high-profile visitors to Wilson's Burn on the hole that had been redesigned as a left-to-right dogleg. It turned out to be the opening round's hardest hole, with Westwood joining 24 other players in failing to make at least a

Marquee Group
The Focus was on Westwood, Woods, Ishikawa

Lee Westwood stepped onto Turnberry's first tee in the opening round and realised he was going to be scrutinised more than in any other tournament he'd ever played. One glance was all it took for the Englishman to realise he was going to play his opening round of The 138th Open Championship under the spotlight.

A phalanx of photographers lined the first fairway as Westwood surveyed the scene in front of him. The horde wasn't there for him. They were there to record the activities of Westwood's playing companions, world number one Tiger Woods and 17-year-old Japanese sensation Ryo Ishikawa.

The trio of Westwood, Woods and Ishikawa was the marquee group of the opening two days. For some, such a three-ball would have been a huge distraction. Not for Westwood. He had the experience to handle the commotion. Besides, any notion that Westwood was the victim of the luck of the draw was false. The Englishman had been consulted about the possibility of playing with Woods and Ishikawa beforehand.

The R&A has never said the opening draw is based on blind luck. Just the contrary, as R&A Chief Executive Peter Dawson admitted.

Japan's Ryo Ishikawa

"The draw is not blind," Dawson said. "We try to take a number of factors into account. As far as we can, we try to pair, or group rather, a North American player with a European player with a rest-of-the-world player. We take into account the requirements or the desires, if you like, of television.

"I was obviously cognisant of the amount of media interest there is in that group. I have spoken to Tiger and to Lee Westwood. They're entirely happy about the grouping."

At times it looked as if there were as many people inside the ropes as outside, as an army of photographers, TV personnel, and journalists followed the group's every move.

Given that Woods is used to such attention, it was perhaps surprising he was the worst player of the group. He returned a one-over-par 71. His play seemed strangely conservative on a day when the course was rendered toothless by the lack of wind. Westwood and Ishikawa, meanwhile, revelled in the hoopla. They returned matching 68s.

"I expected it to be busy out there and there to be a fair bit of activity," Westwood said. "I enjoy playing with Tiger and I enjoyed playing with Ryo, as well. It's nice to have a gallery and some atmosphere out there."

—Alistair Tait

bogey. Woods got up and down from near the 17th tee for a 5, but while Westwood's 68 might have been better, Tiger's 71 could have been worse. He continually had to save himself after going offline, most usually to the right, although his first bogey at the third, after a birdie at the second, was the result of a pull. Both clubs and oaths littered the air as Woods was clearly unhappy with his game.

"I made a few mistakes," Woods said. "I need to clean it up and get myself headed in the right direction. On the 16th I hit a 5-iron and was trying to play about 20 feet left of the hole and the ball landed about 15 feet right of the hole. Not a very good shot."

Ishikawa, who had won three times in Japan including a maiden victory as an amateur, impressed both Woods and Westwood and matched the latter with a 68.

Like Westwood, Graeme McDowell got to three under but ended up with a 68. Twice the first-round leader in the three previous Opens, the Northern Irishman was content to build a challenge over

Low Scores

Low First Nine	
David Howell	31
Miguel Angel Jimenez	31
Paul Casey	31
Low Second Nine	
Kenichi Kuboya	30
Low Round	
Miguel Angel Jimenez	64

Round One Hole Summary

HOLE	PAR	YARDS	EAGLES	BIRDIES	PARS	BOGEYS	D.BOGEYS	HIGHER	RANK	AVERAGE
1	4	354	0	24	113	19	0	0	15	3.97
2	4	428	0	11	116	24	3	2	9	4.17
3	4	489	0	14	104	33	4	1	7	4.19
4	3	166	0	29	104	19	2	2	14	3.01
5	4	474	0	21	87	42	6	0	4	4.21
6	3	231	0	9	111	32	4	0	6	3.20
7	5	538	9	82	55	9	1	0	18	4.43
8	4	454	0	15	105	30	5	1	8	4.18
9	4	449	0	11	107	33	5	0	5	4.21
OUT	**35**	**3,583**	**9**	**216**	**902**	**241**	**30**	**6**		**35.56**
10	4	456	0	17	102	32	4	1	9	4.17
11	3	175	0	23	118	15	0	0	16	2.95
12	4	451	0	14	103	31	7	1	3	4.22
13	4	410	0	27	103	19	6	1	12	4.05
14	4	448	0	15	97	36	8	0	2	4.24
15	3	206	0	17	112	18	8	1	11	3.13
16	4	455	0	24	87	20	22	3	1	4.32
17	5	559	6	78	60	10	2	0	17	4.51
18	4	461	0	31	92	30	2	1	13	4.04
IN	**35**	**3,621**	**6**	**246**	**874**	**211**	**59**	**8**		**35.62**
TOTAL	**70**	**7,204**	**15**	**462**	**1,776**	**452**	**89**	**14**		**71.19**

Mike Weir consulted with caddie Brennan Little.

the weekend rather than lead from the front. "I've tried that and it doesn't work," he reasoned.

Following a trend, both David Howell and Paul Casey, the world number three, went out in 31, four under, Casey after an eagle at the seventh, but fell back to two under. For Howell, it represented a welcome return to form. Recently, he had other things on his mind, like getting married and, on the Tuesday of Open week, making his debut as an after-dinner speaker with a self-deprecating but entertaining performance in front of 270 golfing folk, media, and officials included. "I used to enjoy talking to the press, but these days this is the only way I can get an audience with you," he said.

Harrington, who had much to tell the media with his 2007 and 2008 triumphs, got off to a modest start with a 69. He had missed the cut in his five previous tournaments on the PGA and European Tours, but the week before he won the Irish PGA

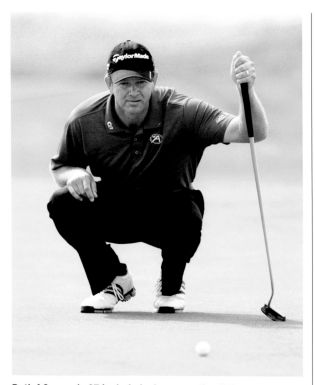
Retief Goosen's 67 included a bogey on the 13th.

Rory McIlroy posted a 69 despite 6 at the eighth.

Championship at The European Club for the third successive year. The Dubliner was struggling to convince himself that he could claim a double hat-trick and so become the first man since Peter Thomson in 1956 to win The Claret Jug three years in a row. He had made a lot of changes to his swing earlier in the year and felt The Open had arrived two weeks early.

At least he was under par, which could not be said for the other hero of Royal Birkdale, Norman. The 1986 Champion at Turnberry had to birdie the last two holes to get in with a 77. "I wasn't feeling confident about the way I was hitting the ball," said the Shark. "The way I drove the ball today was probably the worst I've driven it in my career, and if you're not hitting fairways here then you're going to struggle. If I play nine holes tomorrow and the rest play 18, I might be okay."

Playing alongside Harrington, there was another disappointed Aussie in the form of Geoff Ogilvy, who had a 75, while Anthony Kim had a 73 after a 9

Padraig Harrington struggled but finished on 69.

Excerpts FROM THE Press

Playing here on the 10th hole, Jimenez was happy about the weather.

at the second hole. He drove into the rough, found a fairway bunker with his second, took three to get out, and was over the green in six. A few holes later the American had to undergo treatment from a physiotherapist on the course for a stiff neck.

This was the sixth round in a Major championship in 2009 that Kim had played with Rory McIlroy, the winner of the Silver Medal in 2007. Now a 20-year-old winner on the European Tour, McIlroy started brightly before having to take an unplayable at the eighth hole. The second favourite behind you-know-who in some book-makers' lists prior to the start, McIlroy came in with a 69, while the third member of the group, Retief Goosen, had a 67 helped by a miraculous bunker shot from an awkward stance at the 17th.

Curtis enjoyed four birdies in the last six holes to tie Watson. Both men won The Open on their first appearance, but Curtis then missed the cut in his next three before top-10 finishes in the last two years. "Having more rounds under my belt on links courses is making me a better player," he said. "You're not meant to win the biggest tournament in the world at your first try. It's just weird that it happened to me."

Jimenez, like Howell and Casey, was out in 31, but he built on that with birdies at the 17th and the 18th, where he holed from over 50 feet. The popular Spaniard got a rousing reception at the last, so there were no hard feelings about him displacing Watson at the top

Round of the Day

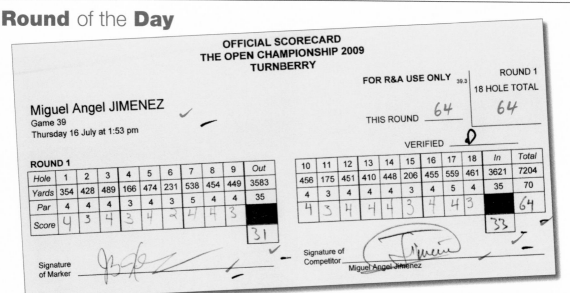

Miguel Angel JIMENEZ
Game 39
Thursday 16 July at 1:53 pm

FOR R&A USE ONLY 39.3

ROUND 1
18 HOLE TOTAL

THIS ROUND 64   64

VERIFIED

ROUND 1

Hole	1	2	3	4	5	6	7	8	9	Out
Yards	354	428	489	166	474	231	538	454	449	3583
Par	4	4	4	3	4	3	5	4	4	35
Score	4	3	4	3	4	2	4	4	3	31

Hole	10	11	12	13	14	15	16	17	18	In	Total
Yards	456	175	451	410	448	206	455	559	461	3621	7204
Par	4	3	4	4	4	3	4	5	4	35	70
Score	4	3	4	4	4	3	4	4	3	33	64

Signature of Marker

Signature of Competitor   Miguel Angel Jimenez

As soon as he awoke, Miguel Angel Jimenez looked out his window towards the sea and knew this would be a good day. "Like a pond, so nice, so calm," Jimenez said. "You can't ask for a better day to play golf. No wind, nothing, and it took care of me."

Jimenez was not off until the afternoon, at 1.53pm in a group with Ian Poulter and JB Holmes, but the conditions held. The weather was perfect. "And then the way I played, the way I hit the ball on the golf course," Jimenez said. He hit the fairway on 12 of the 14 driving holes, missing only "by one metre on the 14th and two metres on the 18th. And also, I had a nice day with the putter, what you need to make a score, no?"

Jimenez's 64, six under-par with no bogeys, was the best score of the day and also his personal best in 17 years of playing in The Open Championship. Twice previously Jimenez had returned 67s, including the third round in 2001, the year he tied for third at Royal Lytham. He was one shot off the first-round lead in 2006 with 67 at Royal Liverpool.

His birdies at Turnberry were on putts of about 12 feet at the second hole, 12 feet at the sixth, 25 feet in two putts at the seventh, eight feet at the ninth, 50 feet in two putts from just off the green at the 17th, and over 50 feet at the 18th hole.

of the leaderboard. "I like very much the Scottish public, the British people," Jimenez said. "They are understanding this sport very well. They appreciate what we are doing. It feels like home.

"I like to play links courses because you need to use your mind," Jimenez added. "It is different from what we're used to playing, no? It is not only getting on the tee and, bang, you put the ball in the air and it stops. You need to have a game plan. You need to avoid the bunkers and keep it on the fairway. But today you could not ask for a better day to play. No wind, nothing, and it took care of me."

Still to finish was Kuboya, the 37-year-old from Japan playing in his second Open. In the last six holes he had not a single par. He birdied the 13th,

Vijay Singh was on 67 with no bogeys.

The 1986 Champion at Turnberry, Greg Norman posted a 77 with birdies on the last two holes.

bogeyed the 14th, and then went on an amazing run that took him into a tie for second place. He birdied the short 15th and then the 16th, eagled the 17th and then birdied the 18th. "I got a good rhythm going and it got better and better as the round went on," he said. "I can't honestly say I like links golf as it can be so difficult. But the result came out good today, so I have to say I like it now."

In the last group of the day, Australia's Terry Pilkadaris and England's Steve Surry, the leader of the Europro Tour, brought the number of sub-par rounds to 50. But The Open record of 63 had not been seriously challenged, and in such good weather Peter Dawson, the Chief Executive of The R&A, was expecting plenty of red figures. But he also knew that once the wind got up the course could take care of itself. "The proof of the pudding concerning the changes to the course was not any of the last three days, but on the Thursday when it was deathly calm and it held up very well," Dawson said. "I knew then that once the wind blew the course would be fine."

But what about Watson? Would he be fine? "So how am I going to do, that's what you all want to know?" Watson asked himself at his post-round press conference. "How am I going to do the next three rounds? Well, I don't know. I don't have a clue what I'm going to do. I wish I could tell you, but we'll have to see what comes."

'I Can Play Links Golf Courses'

By Mike Aitken

If experience of the Scottish links, in general, and Turnberry, in particular, was going to count for something during the 138th staging of The Open on the Ailsa course, then it was little wonder Tom Watson guessed age might not deter him from diving into a deep pool of memories in south Ayrshire which swam all the way back to 1977 and the Duel in the Sun with Jack Nicklaus.

Even before boarding the aeroplane to Scotland, Watson believed, a few weeks shy of his 60th birthday, he understood the challenge of the seaside game and the nuances of Turnberry as well as anyone else in the field. For a start he had played in all the Championships organised at Turnberry by The R&A. There were three previous stagings of The Open in 1977, 1986 and 1994, as well as The Senior Open in 2003 and 2006. And his record of first, 35th, 11th, first and 23rd was more than good enough to inspire confidence.

In spite of taking 83 in the second round of the Masters in April and departing Augusta on the heavy mark of 13 over-par, Watson was convinced he had the game to make an impact in the most egalitarian of Major championships. While the three American Majors are primarily tests of unvarnished power, The Open at Turnberry would be different and decided by accuracy and shotmaking.

Watson's optimism was based on reason rather than emotion. Before he teed-up on Thursday morning, the man from Kansas City, Missouri, had played 107 rounds of links golf in 31 stagings of The Open dating back to his debut triumph in 1975. With a scoring average over 34 years of just over 72, Watson had finished in the top five on no fewer than seven occasions. And, as recently as 2003 at Royal St George's (when he was 53), he had signed off with 69 and finished tied for 18th.

"I can play links golf courses," he observed. "I can get the ball running and I can hit the proper shots into the greens. The greens here are designed so you can roll the ball on them. You can bounce it and there are methods of getting the ball to the hole other than in the air; it's designed that way. I have a belief in myself that I can still do that. And if I'm hitting on all cylinders, I can make a run. I believe in that. That was my belief factor back then in my ability. And it still remains today."

Moreover, Watson felt at home in Scotland. He had won four of his five Opens there as well as all three of his Senior Opens. The American admired the honesty and the kindness of the locals, even if after four decades the Scottish burr still left him scratching his head. And the Scots held Watson in the same esteem they had reserved for Nicklaus and Bobby Jones.

His love affair with Scotland and the Scots had begun 34 years earlier on the morning before the fourth round of The Open at Carnoustie. "A little girl, a next door neighbour to where we had rented a house in Monifieth, came over and gave me an aluminium foil with some heather," Watson recalled. "She said: 'This is for good luck.' Our neighbours didn't want to bother us, and after I won the Championship they reluctantly came over and knocked on the door, wanted to say hello and let me know they were really happy for me. That's the way it started, and that's the way it's always been.

"Any professional golfer who doesn't feel a kindred spirit here in Scotland probably doesn't have an understanding of the game," Watson said. "If you're a professional golfer and you play the game for a living, it's the fabric of your life. And it's the fabric of life over here. People understand the game, even if they don't play it. That's the beauty of it here. That's why I love it."

Few athletes can combine the glory of performance with the eloquence of reflection, but Watson is one of them. You could hear a pin drop at the par-5 seventh on Thursday morning when he faced a bunker shot from a greenside trap of such finesse the flight of the ball needed to take off vertically like a Harrier jump jet. Only when he executed a Hoganesque escape from the sand did the Scottish galleries, already captivated by the romance of such an emotive performance from the veteran, burst into sustained applause.

A couple of hours later, after signing for a 65 which positioned him one stroke off the lead, Watson made his way to the interview room in the media tent where a gathering of sports reporters and golf correspondents from around the world were equally respectful. The game's chroniclers were hushed and hung on Watson's every word.

It was already becoming clear that the story of The Open concerned the continuing competitiveness of the greatest links golfer of all time. In spite of enduring a hip replacement and the burden of 59 summers, Watson still brought vivacity and a sense of joy to the golfer's workplace. When he looked out towards Ailsa Craig and the famous lighthouse, the past Champion smiled, saying: "I love my office."

Tiger's Five Over and Out

By Andy Farrell

Conditions were more severe as Tiger Woods went five over-par to miss the cut, and Tom Watson shared the lead at five under.

When the wind switches direction at Turnberry the Ailsa course becomes a different test of golf. After the calm of Thursday, Friday dawned rainy and cool, with the wind picking up and coming from the north. Suddenly, the examination was even more severe. Ben Curtis, after a birdie at the first to tie for the lead, then dropped eight strokes in the next eight holes to be out in 42. Ian Poulter, Paul Casey, and Geoff Ogilvy all went to the turn in 41. Miguel Angel Jimenez, the overnight leader, bogeyed the second, the third, the fourth and the sixth, where he fluffed a recovery shot in a pot bunker and left it in the sand.

During the first round the front nine was marginally the easier of the two. On Friday it played over a stroke harder than the second half of the course.

Tiger Woods left Turnberry having hit only 15 fairways and 21 greens for a 145 total which tied him for 74th place.

Holes like the second and the run from the fourth to the eighth were into a wind of between 15 and 25mph, with higher gusts out by the lighthouse where the holes around the turn, the ninth, 10th and 11th, were now into a crosswind. This was no gale, as at Royal Birkdale in 2008, but a subtle change that left many struggling to adapt.

Two players with the initials TW both had 5s beside their names by the close of play. One was five under and sharing the lead, the other was five over and sharing a premature departure with all those who missed the cut. However, somewhat surprisingly it was the world number one Tiger Woods who was packing his bags early and Tom Watson showing that whilst consistency and an ability to compete at the top level may dissipate with advancing years, class remains permanent. Watson was meant to be here on a nostalgia trip, reliving the memories of the Duel in the Sun 32 years ago and preparing to bow out of The Open Championship at the age of 60 at St Andrews in a year's time, right? Wrong, again. Watson was once more on top of the leaderboard.

Watson was one of two surprise leaders, the other

2

Excerpts
FROM THE Press

"Five of Ireland's seven players survived the cut, with Graeme McDowell — despite slipping to a 73 for 141 and bemoaning what he termed some 'ridiculous' pin positions — heading the challenge. Darren Clarke and Paul McGinley reached the mid-point on 142, and Padraig Harrington and Rory McIlroy, on 143, also survived for the business end of the Championship."

—Philip Reid, *The Irish Times*

"In one unforgettable hour, as nostalgia gave way to disbelief, Tom Watson and Tiger Woods walked off the 18th green at Turnberry headed in opposite directions few could have imagined. The oldest player at The Open was leading. The best player was leaving. Even a tournament that has been around for 149 years can still serve up a shock or two."

—Doug Ferguson, *The Associated Press*

"Time-worn themes and conventional wisdom about how to succeed in The 138th Open Championship shifted faster than the weather on the Ayrshire coast, and the names on the leaderboard did the same."

—Larry Dorman, *The New York Times*

"Tom Watson's inspirational start at Turnberry this week echoed memories of last year's Open at Royal Birkdale where Australian Greg Norman, at the age of 53, also overshadowed the game's best players."

—Mark Lamport-Stokes, *Reuters*

With Ailsa Craig on the horizon, Tom Watson prepared to putt on the second hole, the first of his five bogeys on the first nine.

being Steve Marino, an American on his first visit to the British Isles and who, including two practice days, had only played four rounds of links golf in his life. And here was Woods missing the cut for the first time at The Open Championship — this was the three-time Champion's 14th appearance (two as an amateur) — and for only the second time as a professional in a Major championship. The only other time was at the US Open in 2006 just weeks after the death of his father.

If there was something not quite right about this picture, then there was a relatively simple explanation. When Peter Dawson, the Chief Executive of The R&A, and his team of expert course design-

Second Round Leaders

HOLE	1	2	3	4	5	6	7	8	9	10	11	12	13	14	15	16	17	18	
PAR	4	4	4	3	4	3	5	4	4	4	3	4	4	4	3	4	5	4	TOTAL
Steve Marino	4	5	3	4	3	2	6	4	4	5	3	4	4	3	3	4	3	4	68-135
Tom Watson	3	5	4	4	5	4	6	4	3	4	2	4	4	3	3	3	5	3	70-135
Mark Calcavecchia	4	5	4	3	5	3	4	4	4	3	3	3	4	3	4	4	5	4	69-136
Ross Fisher	4	4	4	2	4	4	5	3	5	4	3	4	4	5	2	3	4	4	68-137
Retief Goosen	3	4	4	3	5	3	5	4	5	4	4	4	3	4	3	3	5	4	70-137
Miguel Angel Jimenez	4	5	5	4	4	4	5	3	5	5	3	3	4	4	3	4	4	4	73-137
Kenichi Kuboya	3	4	4	2	5	3	5	4	5	4	3	4	6	4	4	4	4	4	72-137
Vijay Singh	4	4	4	2	4	5	4	5	4	5	3	4	4	5	3	3	3	4	70-137
JB Holmes	4	4	4	2	5	3	4	5	5	4	3	4	4	4	2	5	4	4	70-138
James Kingston	5	5	4	2	4	4	4	4	5	4	3	5	4	4	2	4	4	4	71-138
Lee Westwood	4	4	4	3	4	3	5	5	4	4	3	4	4	4	2	5	4	4	70-138
Stewart Cink	4	4	4	5	5	3	4	3	5	4	4	4	4	4	4	3	4	4	72-138
Mathew Goggin	4	4	4	4	4	3	5	5	5	4	3	4	4	4	3	4	4	4	72-138

ers and agronomists suggested some improvements to the Ailsa course prior to the 2009 Open, they were intent on putting more of an emphasis on driving the ball well. After two rounds of the Championship it was obvious this requirement, not always high on the priority list at many Tour courses, was essential for any potential contender.

"The one thing I'm doing very well is I'm putting the ball in the fairway," Watson said. "I'm getting the ball in play off the tee and that's what you have to do here. The players that are struggling are the people that are not finding the fairway. I've played links golf when I'm not playing very well and it's a struggle. You add a little wind like we had today and it's even more of a struggle. How do you get the ball in play?

Ross Fisher returned a 68 with three birdies in a row from the 15th.

"

"It was tricky out there. You had to stay patient. Birdies were very difficult."

—**Ross Fisher**

"I'm getting the ball in play off the tee. And that's what you have to do here."

—**Tom Watson**

"I knew the front nine was going to be playing hard. I saw the scores and I just wanted to stay away from big numbers."

—**Mark Calcavecchia**

"It suited me to have tough conditions today. I had nothing to lose after being six over yesterday. So I'm delighted with that (67) round."

—**Daniel Gaunt**

"I'm pleased with the way I finished, not very pleased with the way I started. You need to put it on the fairways, and I was missing the fairways."

—**Miguel Angel Jimenez**

"You can't allow a birdie followed by a bogey unfortunately. The last six birdies I've made, I've followed the next immediate hole with a bogey."

—**Colin Montgomerie**

"

Mark Calcavecchia chatted with starter Ivor Robson (left) on the first tee.

When you are not confident and hitting it sideways, it gets to you. I don't care who you are, it gets to you."

Over the two rounds, Watson had found 21 of the 28 fairways and was ranked ninth in that category, which was led on 24 by Ross Fisher (tied fourth at three under), Lee Westwood (tied ninth at two under), and Ernie Els (at one over-par, mainly thanks to being ranked 138th in the putting statistics). Watson was also tied second in greens in regulation with 28 out of 36, two behind Mark Calcavecchia, who was in third place at four under.

Woods, on the other hand, had hit only 15 fairways in two days (94th out of the field) and 21 greens (98th), which had a lot to do with him being tied for 74th place, after rounds of 71 and 74, and one outside the cut line which fell at four over-par. Woods was superbly consistent off the tee in winning The Open at Royal Liverpool in 2006, when he only used the driver once during the week, but more often than not manages to get away with his wayward tee balls thanks to his miraculous powers of recovery and courses which do not always punish his worst excesses. This was one that did.

Playing alongside Westwood, who had the advantage of having played a practice round in this wind during the week of the Scottish Open, the contrast was stark. Westwood was playing steady golf and a 70 left him in good shape at two under. "It was a day for patience and grinding out the pars," he said. "You don't often see Tiger hit some of the shots he did today, but everybody is entitled to a bad day every now and again. This is a very demanding course."

A birdie at the seventh put Woods one under for the day and level

Friday Weather

Northerly breeze freshening throughout the day with some heavy showers. Winds north at 10-15mph, gusts to 15-20mph.

A round of level-par 70 gave Lee Westwood a share of ninth place on 138, three strokes behind.

for the Championship, which with other players moving backwards was looking like an increasingly strong position. Bogeys followed at the next two holes, but the real damage was only about to start. At the 10th, a hole that played as a drive and a pitch on Thursday but was now a drive and a long iron, Woods lost his drive in the right rough. Despite the help of the gallery the ball could not be found. As on the first hole at Royal St George's in 2003, Tiger had to march back to the tee. He took a double-bogey, but at the 12th drove into a fairway bunker and made a 5. He was now five over-par and in danger of missing the cut. A hole later he was certain of it after a double-bogey at the 13th which included the ignominy of having a chip beside the raised green return to his feet.

Woods managed birdies at the 16th and the 17th to get back to five over. Although the cut line had risen steadily all afternoon, it refused to budge high enough to include Tiger. "I was right in there in the Championship after seven holes but then had some tough holes and couldn't get it back," Woods said. "I kept compounding my problems out there. I hit some bad tee shots, a couple of bad iron shots, didn't

It's a **Fact**

There were big variations between the scores in the first and second rounds among several of the under-par scorers on the opening day. Ben Curtis went from 65 to 80, John Senden, from 66 to 80, Terry Pilkadaris, from 68 to 82, and Steve Surry, from 69 to 81.
None came close to the record for the biggest variation between two rounds — 20 strokes by RG French (71 to 91) in 1938 and by Colin Montgomerie (64 to 84) in 2002.

'It's been a fantastic day,' said Matteo Manassero. 'It's one of the greatest days of my life.'

Justin Rose's score went from 69 to 72.

get it up and down. You have to play clean to win a Major championship and I haven't done that."

So for the second year running, the Championship would be without the world number one on the weekend. The man who benefited in 2008, when Woods had his knee operation, was Padraig Harrington, winning for the second successive time. But a hat-trick of titles became highly unlikely when the Irishman struggled to a 74 and three over-par. Paul Casey, who entered the Championship as the world number three and with accompanying high expectations, had a 76 and at four over only just squeezed in for the weekend. His first duty then was to get his driver re-shafted after he admitted taking out his front-nine frustrations, which included missing a tap-in at the fifth, on the implement. "It's lasted four years so it's had a good innings," he said.

Among those joining Woods in an early exit were

Matteo Claims Silver Medal

Amateur Champion matches Watson's 70 in second round

The Open often throws up outstanding groupings, but it is doubtful if anyone could have realised quite how outstanding would be the trio that teed-off at 7.58am on the first day and 1.09pm on the second and what an impact on the Championship two of these three men would make. Tom Watson, 59, the oldest man in the field, was accompanied by Matteo Manassero who, at only three months past his 16th birthday, was the youngest. Sergio Garcia, 29, was the third member of the group.

For once, it was not Watson nor Garcia, the professionals, but the young amateur who got most of the admiring stares initially. Manassero arrived at Turnberry having become the youngest winner of The Amateur when he beat England's Sam Hutsby 4 & 3 in the final at Formby one month earlier. John Beharrell at Royal Troon in 1956 and Bobby Cole at Carnoustie in 1966 were both 18. It is said that

noticing how policemen get younger is a sure sign of advancing years, but how about noticing how much younger golfers are becoming?

Manassero had been very good at Formby where he was down only twice in the entire event. But what struck those who watched him closely was that in an era when players seem to take longer and longer to prepare their shots, Manassero appeared to do little more than walk to his ball, quickly choose a club, take up the address, and hit the ball and start walking after it. At Formby he and Hutsby took 3 hours and 10 minutes in the morning 18 holes and 2½ hours for 15 holes in the afternoon.

Still, the final of The Amateur in front of a few hundred spectators is one thing. Playing with one of the game's greatest exponents of links play, a man who had won five Opens and was only one stroke off the lead after the first round, while television was beaming pictures of their progress around the world was quite another.

But just as Watson had made his young playing partner feel at home in the first round, even while outscoring him by six strokes, a 65 to a 71, so he continued to do so in the second, when they each went round in 70.

Manassero's 36-hole total of 141, one over-par, made sure that he made the cut, and as the only amateur to do so he was assured of the Silver Medal. "I'll remember this day for a long time," he said.

Watson had been struck by Manassero's putting on the first day and was even more struck by his play on the second.

"He's a beautiful putter but he is also a great striker of the ball," Watson said. "I was very impressed with him. In fact, I told him on our way down the 18th hole: 'Don't change anything. Just keep enjoying the game and you'll get there.'"

—John Hopkins

Adam Scott, Anthony Kim, and David Duval, who could not repeat his form from the US Open where he was one of the runners-up. Golf's newest knight, Sir Nick Faldo, also missed the cut, along with Greg Norman, Geoff Ogilvy, and Ian Poulter. The Saltman brothers, Elliot and Lloyd, from Edinburgh became the first brothers to play in The Open since the Ozakis in 1992 and the first both to qualify since Manuel and Seve Ballesteros in the mid-70s, also bowed out. Elliot, the elder, was on six over, and Lloyd, the winner of the Silver Medal at St Andrews in 2005, on 12 over.

Someone who might have been expecting to miss the cut after an opening 76 was Daniel Gaunt, an Australian based in London and trying to play the EuroPro Tour as well as work for an equipment company. Just before making it through Local Final Qualifying, Gaunt was intent on giving up on professional golf. But a 67, the lowest score of the day, out in the second group on Friday, guaranteed him two more rounds, and by the end of the week the 30-year-old was

Low Scores	
Low First Nine	
Daniel Gaunt	34
Fredrik Jacobson	34
Fredrik Andersson Hed	34
Yuta Ikeda	34
Raphael Jacquelin	34
Low Second Nine	
Martin Kaymer	32
Ryuji Imada	32
Davis Love III	32
Tom Watson	32
Low Round	
Daniel Gaunt	67

Viewing his lie on the third, Retief Goosen returned a 70.

Miguel Angel Jimenez took two from the bunker at the sixth.

promising to continue living the dream. It helped holing a putt from 40 feet down the slope at the eighth and then chipping in for another birdie at the ninth. His only dropped shot came at the first, and on a day when his peers were throwing them around like confetti this was quite some achievement. Perhaps something had rubbed off from practice rounds with Watson and John Daly.

Curtis was the first of those high up on the first day to play on Friday and went from tied for second to missing the cut after an 80, 15 strokes higher than on Thursday. Jimenez managed to steady himself on the back nine and came home in 34 to be three under. Kenichi Kuboya, the late finisher on Thursday, began well on Friday with a birdie at the first and another at the fourth to reach seven under-par and briefly lead by two strokes. He immediately gave one of those shots back, but a

Round of the Day

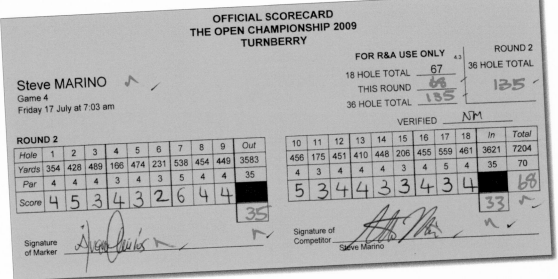

Steve MARINO
Game 4
Friday 17 July at 7:03 am

FOR R&A USE ONLY		ROUND 2
18 HOLE TOTAL	67	36 HOLE TOTAL
THIS ROUND	68	135
36 HOLE TOTAL	135	

VERIFIED _____ NM

ROUND 2

Hole	1	2	3	4	5	6	7	8	9	Out
Yards	354	428	489	166	474	231	538	454	449	3583
Par	4	4	4	3	4	3	5	4	4	35
Score	4	5	3	4	3	2	6	4	4	35

Hole	10	11	12	13	14	15	16	17	18	In	Total
Yards	456	175	451	410	448	206	455	559	461	3621	7204
Par	4	3	4	4	4	3	4	5	4	35	70
Score	5	3	4	4	3	3	4	3	4	33	68

Signature of Marker

Signature of Competitor
Steve Marino

Steve Marino, the co-leader after returning a 68 in the second round, was blunt in reviewing his card. "I really don't think I could have shot one stroke less today, to be honest with you," said Marino, a 29-year-old American who got in The Open as a reserve.

"It was probably one of the best scoring rounds I've ever had," Marino said. "I was really struggling off the tee. I hit it in the rough a bunch, missed a bunch of greens. I holed a shot from 116 yards for a birdie, made a bunker shot for a birdie, and there were points in the round when I felt like I was one-putting every hole."

He ranked first with 51 putts after two rounds, four fewer than the next best total. Conversely, Marino ranked 94th in hitting fairways and 98th in hitting greens in regulation strokes.

Marino balanced three birdies against three bogeys in the first seven holes, including the sand wedge he holed from 116 yards for birdie at the third. He birdied from 30 feet at the fifth and holed out from a bunker for birdie at the sixth. Another bogey came at the 10th, but Marino birded the 14th from 15 feet and made eagle-3 on the 17th from 20 feet.

In the fourth group off in the morning, Marino found harsher conditions in the wind and rain than on the mild opening day. "It was like a totally different golf course," he said. "It was one of the hardest courses I've ever played today."

---

72 also left him at three under, alongside Jimenez, Fisher, Retief Goosen, and Vijay Singh.

Fisher, playing alongside Curtis, had birdied the last three holes on Thursday and on Friday birdied three in a row from the 15th. He was the only player who had scored par or better on the first day to improve his score on the second, following a 69 with a 68. Fisher, who had won twice on the European Tour, is known as a fine driver of the ball, long and straight, but his putting had deserted him when he had a chance to win the US Open at Bethpage the previous month. He finished fifth there and was continuing his good form at Turnberry despite the fact that his wife, Jo, was overdue with their first child.

Kenichi Kuboya was in the lead briefly.

Daniel Gaunt's 67 was the low score of the second day.

With a bogey at 18, Colin Montgomerie missed the cut.

He had a private aeroplane on standby at Prestwick Airport to take him back down to Surrey the moment his wife went into labour, but was perhaps secretly hoping he could be holding The Claret Jug as well as a newborn in a few days' time. "Maybe this is an inspiration, perhaps it is driving me on to hopefully win a Major championship and then see Jo give birth to our first child. It would be a fairytale but obviously it is out of my hands. Hopefully it will hold off for another couple of days and I can play two more good rounds."

The clubhouse leader virtually all day after going out in the fourth group was Marino, a 29-year-old from Oklahoma, now living in Florida and playing in his first Open. He was in his third season on the PGA Tour and in May had lost to Steve Stricker in a playoff at the Crowne Plaza Invitational at Colonial. He was the exception to the rule about having to drive the ball well. "I was really struggling off the tee," he said. "I hit it in the rough a bunch, missed a bunch of greens. I holed a shot from 116 yards for a birdie, made a bunker shot for a birdie, and there were points in the round when I felt like I was one-putting every hole."

Indeed, no one could match Marino's 22 putts for the round, but at times he didn't even need to get the putter out of his bag. At the third, after finding the rough off the tee, he holed out with

Steve Marino posted a 68 with a putt from 20 feet for eagle-3 on the 17th.

"Instead of the predicted Tiger Woods Open, this Turnberry caper is now for the Steve Who? Championship. While an alarmed-looking Woods battled to save pride and his weekend place, Steve Marino was back at his digs watching television and contemplating the ongoing daftness of life, the universe and, especially, Ayrshire."

—**Bill Elliott,** *The Guardian*

"Following his first round in which he shot 67 on the defenceless Ailsa course and planted himself near the top of The Open leaderboard on Thursday, Mark Calcavecchia said his thought of winning the oldest Major in golf went out the window years ago. The 1989 Champion at Royal Troon might want to open the shades anew."

—**Steve DiMeglio,** *USA Today*

"Steve Marino, the accidental tourist, insisted he wasn't at all overwhelmed by the wind-blown, mind-blowing events of his whirlwind trip to Scotland. Evidence suggests he isn't fibbing. 'No, I'm not in a daze,' he said. 'I know what's going on.'"

—**Steve Elling, CBS Sports.com**

"Miguel Angel Jimenez and Ben Curtis took advantage of an Old Lady on Thursday. Yesterday morning she got up in a hellish mood with the rolling pin in hand and exacted the ultimate revenge on her chief assailants."

—**Craig Swan,** *Daily Record*

Three and four shots off the lead were (clockwise from top left): Angel Cabrera (70–139), JB Holmes (70–138), Martin Kaymer (70–139), and James Kingston (71–138).

a wedge shot for a birdie, and at the short sixth he holed out from the bunker short right of the green for a 2. He also made one of only two birdies all day at the fifth, which was the hardest hole of the day, when he hit a 4-iron to 30 feet and, of course, rolled that one in.

Marino did not even know he was going to be playing at Turnberry when he went to the John Deere Classic in Illinois the previous week. When Phil Mickelson officially withdrew and he became the first reserve, he had to get his father to fly from Virginia to Marino's home in Florida and send his passport by express to the John Deere tournament so he could catch the charter on the Sunday night directly to Prestwick. Marino was also lacking in warm clothing but his manager was helping out there.

"Today was so different from yesterday," Marino said. "It was one of the hardest courses I've ever played today but I love the challenge it presents. It's awesome, I'm really enjoying it and having a blast. I've watched this tournament on television my whole life and seen

Third Time Not a Charm

You don't turn up at a Major championship looking for your game — you bring it with you. Padraig Harrington can attest to the veracity of that statement.

The game the defending Champion took to Turnberry was a shadow of the one that had him win a second consecutive Open Championship a year earlier. The Irishman was seeking to do what no player had done since Peter Thomson in 1956 and what only four men had done previously: win three consecutive Opens.

The Dubliner might have pulled off the "three-peat" had he not been in the midst of major swing changes.

Harrington turned up at Turnberry on the back of five missed cuts in PGA Tour and European Tour events. However, he had won the previous week's Irish PGA Championship at The European Club, a formula he'd employed in winning his two previous Opens. If he was hoping it would prove to be the missing ingredient after a dismal year, then he was sadly mistaken.

After rounds of 69 and 74, Harrington was three over-par and eight shots off the lead held by Tom Watson and Steve Marino. Normally eight shots over two rounds wouldn't have fazed Harrington, but so low was his confidence that he could only resort to fantasy scenarios.

"I am hoping just to sneak in on the cut line, to get out nice and early tomorrow morning, in beautiful sunshine, shoot a good score and then the weather to come in," Harrington said before adding the line that underscored his lack of confidence. "We can always dream, can't we?"

Hardly the words of a man feeling on the verge of winning a third Claret Jug, and for good reason. Renowned as one of the hardest workers in professional golf, the Irishman had perhaps put too much work into his game in the run-up to Turnberry. No wonder he bemoaned his groundwork before the Championship.

"My preparation wasn't great," Harrington said. "I wish it was better now. I've changed three things in my backswing and three things on my downswing, and I started off trying to change one. The problem is you change one thing and something else needs to go with it. I think some of the stuff I worked on here at the start of the week definitely could be the

last piece of the jigsaw in what I've been trying to do."

The Irishman made the cut but he was too far off the pace to have any real impact on the Championship. This was one puzzle Harrington never solved.

—Alistair Tait

some crazy things go on. I've got it into my head that some crazy things might happen to me, both good and bad."

Stewart Cink was attuned to the same notion after his trip to Ireland the previous week when he had played at Lahinch, Ballybunion, and Doonbeg. A second round of 72 left the American at two under-par and sharing ninth place with Westwood and others. This was more what he was used to. "I don't think I shot one round last week better than two or three over-par in four days," he explained. "It was blowing like crazy. I shot high scores, made some bad numbers on holes. You would think I came here a little frustrated or questionable, but I came here knowing that, hey, this is what you get when you play links. So I was ready to go."

So a double-bogey-5 at the short fourth did not concern Cink overly, although he also bogeyed the next, but twice in the round he

Second Round Scores	
Players Under Par	7
Players At Par	16
Players Over Par	132

On the ninth tee, Stewart Cink was in contention for the second time in five Opens played.

Lucas Glover missed the cut.

claimed back-to-back birdies, at the seventh and eighth and at the 16th and 17th holes. Having missed the cut in three of his previous four visits to The Open, to be in contention as he was at Carnoustie in 2007 was a reward for his preparations. "I think there is a correlation," he said. "I think I'll definitely be going to play links golf before The Open again, and hopefully my wife and kids will want to accompany me again."

Calcavecchia had his wife Brenda caddieing for him and the team was in good form again as he joined Marino and Fisher as the only players with two sub-par rounds. A 69 had him just one off the lead. No one had found more greens in regulation. "I'm actually kind of using my head, which is unusual," he said. "I'm just trying to hit the greens. It's working so far. This is only about the second time all year I haven't had to struggle to make the cut. I'm usually choking so bad coming down the last few holes on a Friday but I felt great today. I'm swinging well and I've got this new driver and, into the wind, it doesn't spin as much as the old one and I can hit these knuckleballs out there. I'm getting it out there pretty long and it's going straight, too."

Watson followed his 65 with a 70 to remain at five under. "Lady

Among the nine past Champions who made the cut were (clockwise from top) Ernie Els, Mark O'Meara, Paul Lawrie, Tom Lehman, and Justin Leonard.

In the Words of the Competitors...

"

"It's hard to see yourself out there getting any shots back. There aren't a lot of opportunities for making birdies."

—Padraig Harrington

"I watched the golf on television this morning and I knew how demanding it was."

—Lee Westwood

"I don't know if the Championship owes me. I am grateful for this Championship and for the way the people here treat me."

—Sergio Garcia

"It was brutal out there today. The pin placements were extremely tough. The way the wind was blowing, it was impossible to get at them."

—John Daly

"I hit my last good shot on the third — yesterday. Seriously, there were no decent golf shots out there."

—Ian Poulter

"I was one under-par after seven holes and was right there in the Championship, then I had a few tough holes right in a row and couldn't get it back."

—Tiger Woods

"

Sergio Garcia, four shots off the lead, gave Tom Watson a pep talk.

Turnberry took her gloves off today," he said. "She had some teeth." Although he birdied the first and the ninth, Watson made five bogeys going out but was four under for the last 11 holes as he came home in 32, matching the best back nine of the day. Sergio Garcia, one of his playing partners, had helped by turning to Watson on the eighth and saying: "Come on, old man."

"It was nice of Sergio to give me a pep talk," Watson said. "I told him I felt like an old man at that point, but I hit two really good shots there and hit two good shots at No 9 and made a putt and that turned my round around. I never gave up hope and I knew it was going to be a little easier going downwind coming home. My thinking was if I could shoot around even-par I'd be right there, and with the help of a couple of no-brainers that's how it turned out."

He holed some extraordinary putts, from 30 feet at the first, 25 feet at the ninth, and 15 feet at the 11th for a 2, but it was at the 16th that things really started to get otherworldly. Faced with a putt of over 50 feet, he rolled it right into the hole. "Honestly, I was glad to have a putt after having a really awkward lie for my second shot and I had a feeling I was going to make that putt. The spirits were with me again."

Moments later, his other playing partner, Matteo Manassero, The Amateur Champion from Italy, also followed him in from long range. "It made me think of playing with Jack Nicklaus at Augusta. Jack made a big curling putt and then I made it right on top of him," Watson said. "Of course, I was the one who was a lot younger then, so the tables turn. It didn't surprise me. Matteo is a beautiful putter and he is also a great striker of the ball. I was very impressed with him. In fact, I told him on our way down the 18th hole: 'Don't change anything. Just keep enjoying the game and you'll get there.'"

Vijay Singh, finishing on 70, celebrated his eagle-3 on the 17th.

Round Two Hole Summary

HOLE	PAR	YARDS	EAGLES	BIRDIES	PARS	BOGEYS	D.BOGEYS	HIGHER	RANK	AVERAGE
1	4	354	0	33	95	27	0	1	16	3.98
2	4	428	0	6	93	53	4	0	6	4.35
3	4	489	0	13	112	31	0	0	13	4.12
4	3	166	0	17	109	25	5	0	13	3.12
5	4	474	0	2	66	71	15	2	1	4.68
6	3	231	0	8	97	42	8	1	7	3.35
7	5	538	1	41	88	21	4	1	17	4.93
8	4	454	0	7	70	70	9	0	4	4.52
9	4	449	0	8	61	80	6	1	3	4.56
OUT	**35**	**3,583**	**1**	**135**	**791**	**420**	**51**	**6**		**37.60**
10	4	456	0	8	73	54	17	4	2	4.59
11	3	175	0	10	126	17	2	1	15	3.09
12	4	451	0	16	100	31	8	1	10	4.22
13	4	410	0	17	95	35	7	1	9	4.23
14	4	448	0	12	93	42	8	0	8	4.30
15	3	206	0	18	107	23	7	0	12	3.12
16	4	455	0	20	104	20	9	2	11	4.16
17	5	559	7	91	49	6	1	1	18	4.39
18	4	461	0	4	94	50	7	0	5	4.39
IN	**35**	**3,621**	**7**	**196**	**841**	**278**	**66**	**10**		**36.49**
TOTAL	**70**	**7,204**	**8**	**331**	**1,632**	**698**	**117**	**16**		**74.09**

2

36   GOOSEN
36   JIMENEZ   137   -4   WATSON T
36   KUBOYA   137   +1   MANASSERO a
                          +2   HANSON
                          +12   JOHNSON D
                          +6   OOSTHUIZEN
Turnberry 2009   www.opengolf.com

Watson kicked up his heel after a birdie from over 60 feet on the 18th to finish on 70 with a share of first place.

The image of the day was the 16-year-old Manassero, who after a 70 made the cut with four strokes to spare and appeared to play with a smile throughout, and the 59-year-old Watson talking animatedly as they walked up the 18th fairway. Then, as the gallery in the grandstands rose to acclaim Watson, the teenager stepped back and joined the applause. When Watson holed another monster putt from over 60 feet the place erupted again. Watson did a little jig, and it really was beginning to get spooky. "At 18, I kind of had the same feeling as at 16," he said. "If I can make it at 16, why can't I make it at 18? And sure enough, it went in."

Now Watson was the oldest player ever to lead a Major championship. Like Norman at Birkdale the year before, he was right in contention. But Watson was trying not to think about what an amazing story was unfolding. "It's like Greg last year, you have to stay in the present, one shot at the time, the old cliché. I have never thought any other way."

But he added: "To be able to be doing what I'm doing, making a few lucky putts here and there and still feeling like I have a chance to win, that's pretty cool at the age of 59. That's why it's kind of spiritual."

Problem after Problem for Woods

By Lewine Mair

Friday afternoon was eerily quiet. There was no shortage of spectators but they were speaking in hushed tones about Tiger Woods' fading chances of making the weekend. With four holes to play, and at a time when it had been more or less established that the cut would come at four over-par, the world number one was seven over.

"Knowing Tiger," said Paul Casey, who was among those to have finished on the four-over mark, "he'll still make it." Woods' old friend Mark O'Meara, on the other hand, was not so sure. As he broke away from some putting practice, the 1998 Open Champion was shaking his head in mingled astonishment and disbelief. "I would have put my house on Tiger being somewhere around the top of the leaderboard at this stage," he said. "When we played together on Tuesday, it struck me that he was hitting the ball every bit as well as when he won his Opens at St Andrews. I just don't know what's up with him."

Woods' Thursday 71 had not caused undue concern. After all, he was only one over-par and neither better nor worse placed than he had been in countless previous events which he had gone on to win. "I thought if I shot under par for the tournament, at the end of the day I would be right there in the Championship, probably in the top 10," he said.

He unleashed the first of several rough-bound tee shots as early as the third hole, where he required a free drop from a television tower. On a slightly different tack, there was a seemingly topped second at the ninth, while, when it came to the 16th, he followed Lee Westwood into the burn. In Woods' case, his 5-iron second did not so much as touch the putting surface before taking a watery dive.

With the wind more of a factor on the Friday, the expectation was that this great golfer would be making his way under par with some of his low stingers. To the surprise of the shot-making connoisseurs, there were none of those, though, in truth, he was getting by well enough without them. After seven holes, he was one under for the day and, to use his own words, "right there ... then I had a few tough holes in a row and couldn't get it back."

That was when he had a rush of mishaps resulting in a run of bogey, bogey, double-bogey, par, bogey, double-bogey. The double at the 10th included a lost ball after his tee shot veered a good 40 yards offline. Some 60 people were involved in the search but, as applied to his lost ball at the first at Royal St George's in 2003, they searched to no avail.

It was at the 13th that the alarm bells sounded loud and clear. Usually, the impression people have of Tiger is of a player who has what it takes no matter the circumstances. Not at the 13th. "I made a double-bogey there from 150 yards," Woods said. "It was just problem after problem. I kept compounding my problems out there."

Woods hit through the green in two before hitting a first chip which dared to come back down the slope. Patently upset, Woods launched into his first putt without walking up to make his usual careful study of the line. Almost immediately after he had holed out for his 6, the cameras caught him taking a long hard look at what he had done. The caption in the *Daily Express* — That sinking feeling — could not have been more apposite.

He made it back to six over-par with a holed 20-footer at the 16th and he picked up a further shot at the 17th following an exquisite little chip from the back of the green. All of which left him tantalisingly placed at five over with one to play.

His tee shot at the 18th was a beauty, while his second looked the part before bounding through the green. The spectators were willing him to make the one more birdie he needed, with a little lad standing beside the green summing up their mood when he said: "I'm no coming tomorrow unless Tiger's here."

Alas, Woods failed to get up and down and his 2009 Open campaign was over with a round of 75. He missed the cut for only the fifth time in his 13 years as a professional and the second time in a Major championship. In his post-round interview, Woods said: "I just made mistakes. You can't make mistakes and expect to not only make the cut but also try to win a championship. You have to play clean rounds of golf, and I didn't. I made my share of mistakes out there and didn't play a very clean card."

Tom Watson put an end to the suggestion that Woods' lapse might be rather more than merely a short-term hiccup. Having agreed that it was surprising that he should have had one shot too many, the old Champion proffered the wisest of explanations: "When you are not confident about where you are hitting it and you start knocking it sideways a few times, it gets to you. I don't care how good you are."

Third Round

History in the Making?

By Andy Farrell

Aiming for a sixth Open title and a stack of other records, overnight leader Tom Watson says: 'This old geezer might have a chance.'

Could he really do it? There were a lot more believers by the end of the third round when the 59-year-old Tom Watson took sole possession of the lead and was only 18 holes away from a record-equalling sixth Open title. It was not so much the fact of Watson leading but the way the round unfolded. Challengers came and fell back again, Watson slipped behind but rallied, birdieing the 16th and 17th holes. Had he faded away it would have been understandable, but this old timer was sticking around.

Watson had his own analysis of the week. "The first day, it was let the old geezer have his day in the sun, you know, a 65," he said. "The second day, you said, that's okay, that's okay. And now today, you kind of perk up your ears and say, this old geezer might have a chance to win the tournament. It's kind of like Greg Norman last year."

With a contented smile, Tom Watson paused on the 18th green.

This was the second year in a row that a former great in his 50s led The Open with a round to play. At Birkdale the 53-year-old Norman was two in front of the field, although one of his closest challengers was Padraig Harrington, who would go on to claim a second successive Claret Jug. What undid Norman, apart from the Irishman's brilliance at closing out the Championship, was not his age but his lack of competitive play over a number of years when injuries and his business kept him off the course.

Watson, fitter than ever after a hip replacement the previous autumn, has always kept playing golf, revelling in trying to compete, and hit quality shots under pressure. The third of his three Senior Open titles came at Muirfield in 2007. By some margin his was the most imposing name on the leaderboard. With Harrington, Tiger Woods and Angel Cabrera, having won nine of the previous 12 Major championships, all out of contention — at least the Argentinean was five strokes behind so could not be totally discounted — this was a prize up for grabs. Why could the old geezer not do it and smash all manner of records?

3

After two bogeys in the first seven holes, Stewart Cink settled down for a round of 71, and finished three strokes behind.

On another difficult day for scoring, with only five players breaking par, Watson's 71 left him at four under-par and one clear of Mathew Goggin, an Australian yet to win in America or Europe, and Ross Fisher, who had become another sentimental favourite due to the dilemma of his wife about to give birth. A further stroke behind were the ominous duo of former double US Open champion Retief Goosen and England's Lee Westwood, who was in form and seemingly getting ever closer to a Major breakthrough.

How far back was too far back? Only seven players were left under par — there had been 50 on the first day — and at one under were Jim Furyk, the 2003 US Open champion, and Stewart Cink, a winner at the World Golf Championship level but no higher. At level-par were Bryce Molder and Thongchai Jaidee. It was Molder, the 30-year-old

former American Walker Cup player, who returned the best score of the day, a 67 with five birdies after two early bogeys. The pattern of each round was again similar to Friday, with shots dropped at the start and recovered later on. The weather was almost identical to the previous day, wet early and sunny later on but for the odd shower, the wind again basically from the north but attacking the course at a marginally new angle.

Molder, who has Poland Syndrome, which means his left hand is much smaller than his right, jumped from a tie for 53rd overnight to a tie for eighth place. There were only four other rounds of 69, moving those players up the leaderboard, particularly Goggin, who made the biggest move within the top 10. Going in the opposite direction, however, were Steve Marino, the co-leader overnight who had a 76 to fall into a tie for 10th, and Mark Calcavecchia, whose

Third Round Leaders

HOLE	1	2	3	4	5	6	7	8	9	10	11	12	13	14	15	16	17	18	TOTAL
PAR	4	4	4	3	4	3	5	4	4	4	3	4	4	4	3	4	5	4	
Tom Watson	4	4	4	3	4	[4]	(4)	4	[5]	4	3	[5]	4	4	[4]	(3)	(4)	4	71-206
Mathew Goggin	4	4	4	3	[5]	3	(4)	[5]	4	4	(2)	4	4	4	3	4	(4)	4	69-207
Ross Fisher	4	4	(3)	3	[5]	3	5	4	4	4	3	[5]	4	[5]	3	(3)	(4)	4	70-207
Lee Westwood	4	4	[5]	3	4	3	5	4	4	4	3	(3)	4	4	3	4	(4)	[5]	70-208
Retief Goosen	4	(3)	4	3	4	3	[7]	4	4	4	3	[5]	4	[5]	3	4	(3)	4	71-208
Jim Furyk	4	4	4	3	4	3	[6]	4	4	4	3	4	(3)	4	[4]	4	(4)	4	70-209
Stewart Cink	4	4	4	3	[5]	3	[6]	4	4	4	(2)	4	4	4	[4]	4	(4)	4	71-209
Bryce Molder	4	4	[5]	3	[5]	3	5	(3)	(3)	4	3	(3)	4	4	(2)	4	(4)	4	67-210
Thongchai Jaidee	4	4	4	3	(3)	3	(4)	4	(3)	[5]	3	4	4	[5]	3	[5]	(4)	4	69-210
Richard S Johnson	4	4	[5]	[4]	(3)	[4]	(4)	[5]	(3)	4	3	4	4	(3)	3	4	(4)	4	69-211
Boo Weekley	4	4	4	3	4	[4]	[6]	(3)	[5]	4	(2)	4	[5]	4	3	4	(4)	[5]	72-211
Angel Cabrera	4	[5]	4	3	[5]	3	5	[5]	4	4	3	4	[5]	4	3	4	(4)	(3)	72-211
Steve Marino	4	[5]	[5]	[4]	[6]	3	(3)	4	4	4	(2)	[5]	4	4	[6]	[6]	(4)	(3)	76-211

Following dropped shots at the third and fifth holes, Bryce Molder ran off five birdies for a 67, the low score of the day.

Round of the **Day**

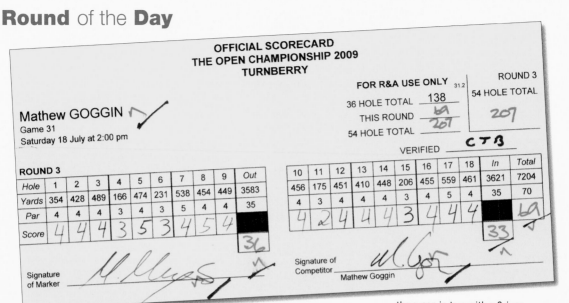

Sometimes it does not take a birdie or even a par to make the biggest difference in a round. In the case of Mathew Goggin in the third round, it was a bogey-5 at the 454-yard eighth hole, which Goggin described as "the turning point of the round for me. I looked like I was going to make a double-bogey, and made a nice putt from around three or four metres there, then I played quite

well after that. The last 10 holes were really solid."

Goggin, who also took bogey at the fifth hole, recorded three birdies in a round of 69 for a 207 total, three under-par, to be tied for second with Ross Fisher, one stroke behind the leader, Tom Watson. His birdies were at the seventh hole after a sand wedge to eight feet, at the 11th with a pitching wedge to six feet, and at the 17th on two putts from 25 feet after reaching

the green in two with a 6-iron.

In his fourth Open, Goggin tied for 46th in 2003 at Royal St George's. He started with a 68 in 2004 at Royal Troon, then returned a 78 to miss the cut. He missed the cut in 2006 at Royal Liverpool, despite posting a 69 in the second round. The 35-year-old Australian plays on the PGA Tour in America. His career-bests were ties for second in both the 2006 Cialis Western Open and 2008 Memorial Tournament.

Third Round Scores	
Players Under Par	5
Players At Par	6
Players Over Par	62

77 meant the former Champion plummeted to a tie for 27th.

Watson and Marino did not tee-off until 3pm and Watson had used the morning profitably to watch some of the early television coverage and get a feel for the course conditions. Marino bogeyed the second to leave Watson ahead on his own, and the younger American proceeded to drop five shots in four holes before rallying with an eagle at the seventh. Watson made five straight pars before bogeying the sixth. Goosen was briefly tied for the lead but only while in the process of taking a double-bogey at the par-5 seventh. His second shot was found in the left rough but he had to take an unplayable and took four to get down from near the eighth tee.

Watson got back to five under with a 4 at the seventh, but three-putted from the back of the ninth green and also three-putted at the 12th. Suddenly he was tied with Goggin, who had just birdied the 17th to get under par for the round and to three under-par for the

Australian Mathew Goggin got himself into Sunday's final game with a 69 to be three under-par.

Championship. Out in one over, the 35-year-old from Tasmania, where he grew up playing in the wind, had an eventful back nine. Getting close to the hole at the short 11th was proving difficult, but he hit a wedge to six feet there for a 2 and went to extraordinary lengths to ensure a par at the 16th. Seeing his second shot fail to settle on the green, he sprinted up the fairway in order to mark the ball in case it trickled off the putting surface towards Wilson's Burn.

"It's a long time since I've run like that," he said. "I was knackered after I did it so it probably wasn't a very good idea. I had an 8-iron shot and was staring it down thinking I had hit a great shot. But when it landed where it did I was a bit shocked. It looked like it wasn't going to stay where it was and so I just had to make sure. But then I was kind of messing around, too."

Out of breath or not, Goggin, who was playing on the weekend at The Open for only the second

A double-bogey on the 18th dropped Henrik Stenson six strokes behind.

Jim Furyk was tied for sixth after his 70.

Francesco Molinari scored eagle-3 on the 17th for a 71.

time, two-putted from 25 feet for a 4 at the par-5 17th and set the clubhouse lead at three under. "The turning point of the round was the eighth, where I looked like making a double after birdieing the seventh. But I knocked in a good putt there for a bogey and played the last 10 holes really solid." It was only later that it would be confirmed that Goggin would be playing alongside Watson on the final day, but the Australian remembered playing with him in the third round at Sandwich in 2003, his best day at an Open before this one. "It was shocking how good he was," Goggin recalled. "It was ridiculous. Such a great player, such a great Champion, he was just smashing it around the course. It was a great experience."

In the pairing ahead of Goggin were Cink and Westwood. The American was prepared for the Englishman to get the crowd's attention, and Westwood rewarded the faithful with a superb 4-iron at the 12th which ran up to less than three feet from the hole. Surely he would hole this one? Westwood had been grinding out the pars, but the birdie putts, since the first three holes of the Championship on Thursday, had been rare. In it went and Westwood was back to level for the round having earlier bogeyed the third. At the next he

Lee Westwood moved this shot only a foot at 18, but salvaged a bogey.

had to get up and down for a par but then he was back in two-putt mode, including from just off the green at the 17th for a birdie-4 to get to three under and into a tie for the lead.

It did not last, because his 8-iron approach at the last was pulled and caught the mound of rough just in front of the green. "Five yards further right and it would have hopped up and given me a 25-footer for birdie," Westwood said. "It was my error for going for the flag. It was one of the few times I slipped away from my game plan of hitting the middle of the greens, being conservative and patient. Just a small error but better today than tomorrow."

Westwood's ball was in a horrid lie and he could only move it a foot with his first effort, but from there he got up and down to limit the damage to a bogey. A 70 left him at two under-par. "Emotionally I feel very calm and the plan is to be patient," he said. "I don't have to think that I have to do too much. I just need to plot my way around the course as I have been and try to finish one in front."

Earlier in the week, Westwood was presented with a glass and silver replica of The Claret Jug as the winner of the Golf Foundation's Spirit of Golf Award. The next day he dearly wanted to claim the

In the Words of the Competitors…

"

"I'll see tomorrow if those two shots (double-bogey on the 18th) would've come in handy. It's obviously disappointing to finish that way."

—Henrik Stenson

"When I finished the practice round on Wednesday, I really felt good about my chances to do well in the tournament. And so far so good."

—Tom Watson

"There's a lesson to be learnt there (at the 18th) because I strayed from my game plan. I hit it straight at the flag. That was the main mistake. If I hit it five yards right of the flag, I would be one shot better."

—Lee Westwood

"I can't strike the ball any better. I created lots of birdie opportunities. I feel it was an opportunity missed today."

—Justin Rose

"There's less guess work on this course than on some of the other Open venues we play."

—Luke Donald

"I love the golf course. I just wish I was playing better."

—Paul Casey

"

Scores of 72 tied Chris Wood (left) for 14th place and Boo Weekley for 10th place.

real thing. Having finished third at the US Open in 2008, playing with Woods and missing the playoff by a single shot, he believed he was ready to win a Major. "I've put myself in position a few times before and I've learnt from those experiences," he said. Westwood's record in The Open had not been all that great, with just two top-10 finishes, but both of them had come in this part of the world, just up the Ayrshire coast at Royal Troon.

For a man who broadcasts his latest news on Twitter, Cink was still flying under the radar. He did have a scare to report, however. "Pretty sure I've got swine flu," he tweeted. "I thought if you like BBQ as much as I do that your antibodies would be built up against it." It turned out he did not have swine flu but he was not feeling great. "It was a worry," he said. "I was feeling really bad and I've been on medication all week."

Cink had his second successive round over par, but a 71 left him at one under and still in touch. He bogeyed the fifth and the seventh, but got a 2 at the 11th and finished with seven 4s, including a bogey at the 15th and a birdie at the 17th. "It's funny over here," he said. "The weather dictates what your score is. I felt like I played the same every day. I've hit the ball well and kept it in play and avoided the

Luke Donald's level-par 70 put him on 213.

Camilo Villegas was on 212 after his 73.

Angel Cabrera birdied 17 and 18 for 72 and 211.

bunkers for the most part. I shot four under the first day and then shot over par the next two. A little bit of wind and it gets a lot trickier.

"But links golf and I really like each other. These weather conditions are absolutely ideal for this kind of golf. Nothing goofy, just the right amount of wind to challenge everybody and see what everybody has. It was a test out there. Everybody stumbles and it's a question of how much you picked yourself up. It wasn't a day where I got everything out of the round, but I think there is still hope."

Three times Cink had finished third in a Major championship, but the one everybody remembers was the US Open in 2001 when he missed a tap-in on the 72nd green thinking he was out of contention. Then Goosen had his own putting miscue

Retief Goosen took 7 here on the seventh, but still tied for fourth.

Richard S Johnson's 69 tied him for 10th.

and, had Cink holed out properly, he would have joined the South African and Mark Brooks in a playoff. Cink had five victories on the PGA Tour and has always been a gritty competitor in Ryder and Presidents Cups, but after The Players Championship in May he had decided to revamp his game, getting rid of the belly putter and almost writing off the rest of the season.

"The second half of last year really stunk and the start of this year I was spluttering," he explained. "I just decided this isn't working any more. I was putting really poorly and that was affecting the rest of my game, the same with any golfer. I decided on a total overhaul, starting with the removal of the long putter. I needed to change my mental outlook, too, because I didn't have much of a pre-shot routine that I could lean on under pressure. So I scrapped everything and went with the short putter.

"I didn't really change my golf swing, although I'm always tinkering. I don't have a game where I need to be dead-on mechanically. I play a lot of feel shots, it's a gut instinct type of golf. When I started putting better, all of a sudden the confidence started coming back. I'm looking forward to being in contention and giving it a go. Apart

One of Cink's three dropped shots came here at the seventh hole.

from Tom Watson, there's a lack of experience on the leaderboard in Majors. I've got experience in Majors, I just haven't won any. I think I'm going to attack the course a bit tomorrow but make sure I keep my composure."

Fisher, who got off to a good start with a birdie at the third but then dropped three shots between the fifth and the 14th, had his now customary good finish with birdies at the 16th and 17th, holes he had birdied all three days. He had actually played the last four holes in eight under for the three rounds. Now, after a 70, he was tied in the clubhouse at three under with Goggin. "I'm delighted with that score because it was another tough day," he said.

Not that his interviewers at the end of the day wanted to know much about his golf, albeit his recent experiences of Bethpage where

Despite a missed birdie on 15, Ross Fisher was tied for second.

His 70 placed Paul McGinley in a tie for 14th on 212.

he was fifth in the US Open made him a genuine contender. But what about the baby news? Wife Jo had not yet gone into labour and he was still planning on "supporting her 100 percent." He added: "It's been a long week, an intriguing week. I've got through three days, she's got through three days. Hopefully, I can hang on for one more day and she can, too."

With Fisher and Westwood together in the penultimate pairing on Sunday, there were high hopes for a first British winner of The Open for 10 years, since Paul Lawrie at Carnoustie, and of a first English winner since Nick Faldo at Muirfield in 1992. "I'm not sure why a British guy has not won The Open," Fisher said. "We've got a tremendous amount of talent in the game. Hopefully that will change

Baby Questions
A dilemma for Ross Fisher intrigues the nation

One of The Open's main sub-plots — whether or not Ross Fisher would leave in a hurry to attend the birth of his first child — was gathering momentum on the third day of the Championship. After all, the baby in question was already four days late.

The night before, Fisher had reiterated that he still intended to withdraw at once if his wife, Jo, were to go into labour. "I want to be with her and I will be with her because this is something I definitely don't want to miss," he said.

How Fisher's dilemma occupied the minds of the radio and television people. For the umpteenth day in a row, listeners and viewers were invited to ring in with their opinions on what is — at least in the United Kingdom — a relatively modern problem. Years ago, wives did not tend to follow their husbands' every step around the golf course any more than husbands kept a constant watching brief over wives in labour.

As you would expect, there were golf followers who thought it was madness that he would even consider leaving Turnberry when he was faring so well — and others who were equally adamant that babies deserved precedence over birdies, whatever the circumstances.

In the event, there were no desperate messages from home to interrupt the 70 which Fisher added to opening scores of 69 and 68. He was playing alongside Mark Calcavecchia, and while the older man was producing a wily brand of golf, hitting under the wind to the middle of greens, he was going for the pin. Out in 35 after making a curly 15-footer for a birdie at the third and dropping a shot at the fifth, he had two birdies at the 16th and 17th to set against two more dropped shots.

That Fisher had by then notched as many as eight birdies over the last four holes during the week must have had him pondering on what such a finish might do for him in the fourth round.

To give a couple of other relevant statistics, Fisher was at that point ranked third alongside Lee Westwood in terms of greens hit in regulation — and equal first in the birdies stakes. Along with Watson and four others, he had notched as many as 13.

On Saturday evening, he was asked one more "baby" question. What would happen if he got the call when he was on the last tee and in the lead? The answer, here, was that he would run all the way down the fairway, seize The Claret Jug and make for home.

Another similarity to rounds two and three lay in his finish: On the first day, he had birdied each of the last three holes. On the second, he birdied the 15th, 16th and 17th. Now, on the Saturday, he birdied each of the 16th and 17th.

All of which would have had him thinking how any one of those three finishes might work well for him on the morrow.

—Lewine Mair

Thongchai Jaidee (far left) had two 69s and was tied for eighth.

Thomas Aiken (left) tied for 14th with his 69.

Excerpts FROM THE Press

"Across from the course he helped make famous is a luxury hotel that sits atop a majestic hill and is quite the sight for golfers heading to the home hole at Turnberry. Inside there is a suite named for Tom Watson, the man who won the first Open Championship here in 1977 after an epic 'Duel in the Sun' with Jack Nicklaus. Guess who's staying in those digs? It is only appropriate that Tom Watson get the room that bears his name."

—Bob Harig, ESPN.com

"Yesterday morning 17 Britons pulled back their curtains in Ayrshire, saw a northwesterly breeze stiffening the flags and the vapour-trail of Tiger Woods' departing jet disappearing in the distance, and knew they had a chance of lifting The Claret Jug."

—Paul Kelso,
The Sunday Telegraph

"The first man to finish set a pace few could match by racing around, alone, in three hours dead. 'I was offered a marker to play with,' said Johan Edfors, 'but I chose to play on my own.'"

—Robert Winder,
The Independent on Sunday

"Seve Ballesteros hopes to play in The Open at St Andrews in 2010, spurred by images of long-time rival Tom Watson leading at Turnberry."

—John David, *Sunday Express*

"John Daly admits he must sort out his putting to have any chance of winning The Claret Jug again."

—Gavin Berry, *Sunday Mail*

Steve Marino took 6 on the par-3 15th after having an unplayable lie.

tomorrow, whether it's myself or Lee or someone else. Playing with Lee will be great fun. Hopefully we can throw a few birdies at each other and try and get our names up at the top of the leaderboard."

Back at the 14th, Watson holed a 20-footer for par, but then found the back bunker at the 15th and dropped a shot to fall out of the lead. But at the 16th, where he had holed an outrageous putt on Friday, he did so again, making a 40-footer before claiming a 4 at the 17th to get back into the lead by one.

Marino was not having such a good time with 6s at the 15th and 16th before closing with two birdies, but it was quite an experience. "It was a combination of the good, the bad and the ugly," he said. "But it was awesome playing with Tom. I told him he could be the King of Scotland. These people love him. It was super special to watch him and, you know, there's a reason he has won five Claret Jugs."

If Watson could make it six he would equal a record set by Harry Vardon as long ago as 1914.

Round Three Hole Summary

HOLE	PAR	YARDS	EAGLES	BIRDIES	PARS	BOGEYS	D.BOGEYS	HIGHER	RANK	AVERAGE
1	4	354	0	5	49	17	2	0	8	4.22
2	4	428	0	4	49	20	0	0	8	4.22
3	4	489	0	3	48	22	0	0	7	4.26
4	3	166	0	5	57	10	1	0	13	3.10
5	4	474	0	6	26	35	6	0	1	4.56
6	3	231	0	6	48	18	1	0	11	3.19
7	5	538	4	20	37	9	3	0	17	4.82
8	4	454	0	4	44	22	3	0	6	4.33
9	4	449	0	10	50	11	2	0	15	4.07
OUT	**35**	**3,583**	**4**	**63**	**408**	**164**	**18**	**0**		**36.77**
10	4	456	0	9	51	11	1	1	13	4.10
11	3	175	0	6	60	7	0	0	16	3.01
12	4	451	0	7	31	30	5	0	2	4.45
13	4	410	0	5	56	11	1	0	12	4.11
14	4	448	0	3	40	27	3	0	3	4.41
15	3	206	0	3	42	24	3	1	3	3.41
16	4	455	0	3	46	17	5	2	3	4.41
17	5	559	4	44	21	4	0	0	18	4.34
18	4	461	0	8	47	14	3	1	10	4.21
IN	**35**	**3,621**	**4**	**88**	**394**	**145**	**21**	**5**		**36.45**
TOTAL	**70**	**7,204**	**8**	**151**	**802**	**309**	**39**	**5**		**73.22**

"I don't know what is going to happen," Watson insisted. "But I do know one thing. I feel good about what I did today. I feel good about my game plan, the number of birdies and bogeys I can make. I didn't feel real nervous out there. I felt serene. Even though I messed up a couple of times, it didn't bother me. The crowd was wonderful on every tee, every green, and the feeling is mutual. So, who knows, it might happen."

Two things needed further elaboration before Watson was allowed to head back up the steps to the hotel, the dining room overlooking the course, and the suite that already bears his name. One was about his putting, so magical this week but with a history of letting him down when it matters. "Every now and then it works, you know," he said. "It's just every now and then. And boy, is it working at the right time right now." The second was whether he would feel nerves the next day. "No, I don't. I feel

Oliver Wilson was on 213 after his 71.

Watson's was the most imposing name on the leaderboard after three rounds.

like my nerves are too well fried to feel them," he said, laughing. "I mean, come on. Let's just go with what I've got. I'm not thinking about that."

What Watson had already achieved was inspiring enough. Take Seve Ballesteros, back home in Spain where he would watch the golf on Sunday after having lunch with Jose Maria Olazabal. While his recovery from treatment for a brain tumour continued, he announced: "After watching Tom Watson the last three days, I want to play at St Andrews next year." And, in Florida, Jack Nicklaus was watching on television and was prompted to send his first ever text message to his old friend and Duel in the Sun rival, even if he had to get his wife Barbara to help him. "Whether or not Tom plays well tomorrow and wins or not, it doesn't make a difference," Nicklaus said. "Of course, we would all love to see Tom win, but what he has already accomplished is a phenomenal achievement."

A Ball-Striker's Paradise
Mathew Goggin found that Turnberry suits his game

While there wasn't much in Mathew Goggin's resumé to suggest he was an Open Champion in waiting — he hadn't won a tournament for 10 years and his best finish in the oldest Major was 46th at Sandwich in 2003 — the Australian never lost faith in his own ability to make a mark on the game. "I believe that if I keep knocking at the door," he said, "it will eventually open for me."

The resilience which typified the Arizona-based golfer's performance over the first three rounds at Turnberry started on Thursday with a stalwart reaction to a frustrating bogey on the first hole. It made him re-focus his efforts, and four birdies over the next seven set up an impressive opening salvo of 66. Although he didn't putt well on Friday, using the blade 36 times in a round of 72, the fact Goggin made light of the tricky crosswinds and found no fewer than 15 of the Ailsa course's greens in regulation figures was a harbinger of things to come. Turnberry was generally regarded as a ball-striker's paradise and Goggin knew how to shape a shot.

When he made eight single putts on Saturday, compared to just one on Friday, it was no surprise to see the 35-year-old from Hobart in Tasmania post a 69 and clamber onto the summit of the leaderboard. His inward half of 32, which included birdies at the 11th and 17th holes, also avoided the blemish of any dropped shots. "I've always hit the ball well enough to be around about," he reflected. "So when the other part of the game starts to match up, that's when you finish up at this end of the leaderboard."

Having missed seven cuts in 17 events on the PGA Tour before travelling to Scotland, Goggin's solid ball-striking over the first three days catapulted him into the eye of the storm and a fourth round pairing in Sunday's final group with Tom Watson. It was one of the biggest challenges of his career, though one he hoped to embrace, bearing in mind he'd previously enjoyed watching a master class first-hand in the company of the five-time Open Champion six years earlier at Sandwich.

"That was probably the highlight of The Open for me, playing with Tom Watson in the third round, because he's such a great player and such a great Champion, especially at The Open," recalled Goggin. "And it was also shocking just how good he was. It was ridiculous. I'm thinking, you know, he's getting on in years and not playing so much and he's just smashing it around this golf course. I was really impressed. He was really good to me and I had a great experience. It was definitely a highlight of The Open for me."

—Mike Aitken

Fourth Round

Cink Ends Watson's Dream

By Andy Farrell

Winning his first Major title in a playoff, Stewart Cink, 36, denied an historic victory for Tom Watson, 59, who missed his chance at the last hole.

Only one name can be added to The Claret Jug every year and beside 2009 it will always say Stewart Cink. That the engraver was poised to add the name of Tom Watson for a sixth time was in itself remarkable and ultimately a bittersweet notion. To lose in the fashion Watson did, bogeying the last and then failing to put up a fight in the playoff, would have been hard for anyone to bear, let alone for an "old fogey," as he put it, of 59 who was about to make history in all manner of ways. But though Watson proved himself here a champion of links golf for all years, The Champion Golfer of *this* year was Cink, a 36-year-old from Georgia claiming his first Major title.

This was an Open Championship with every bit

as much drama as on Turnberry's first outing as host in 1977. There were more characters involved this time than last, when Watson and Jack Nicklaus duelled alone. Six players held the lead during the afternoon and Cink was the sixth and last of them. Timing is everything. But not before Watson, as 32 years before, had birdied the 71st hole to go one up with one to play.

Back then, Nicklaus birdied the last and Watson followed him in. Here it was Cink who claimed a 72nd hole birdie, from 16 feet, while others — first Chris Wood, then Lee Westwood, and finally, and most desperately, Watson — bogeyed it. "It will be the most crucial putt I've ever struck in my life," Cink said. It got him into the four-hole playoff with Watson, and with the older man running out of steam, Cink ruthlessly took control, six strokes ahead, by 14 to Watson's 20, when they finished on the 18th for the second time.

In truth, the extra time, rather than adding to the spectacle, was uncomfortable to watch, the deflation following Watson's dribbled attempt at an eight-foot Championship winning putt at the 72nd hole as acute as most observers had ever

Stewart Cink read the names on The Claret Jug as Tom Watson looked on.

4

Lee Westwood missed from six feet on the 18th.

Tom Watson missed there from eight feet.

experienced. That Cink, who three times previously had finished third in Majors, was good enough to put himself in position to take advantage hardly made him the villain of the piece. But under the circumstances of Watson's demise, any other winner, even someone else with the TW initials, Tiger Woods, or a British winner, and both Wood and Westwood also left with regrets, it was hard not to think this plot had a twist too many.

"It would have been a hell of a story, wouldn't it?" Watson agreed. "It wasn't to be. And, yes, it's a great disappointment. It tears at your gut, as it has always torn at my gut. It's not easy to take. I put myself into position to win and didn't do it on the last hole. I knew I was playing well coming in and I could have dreamt it, yes. And it was almost. Almost. The dream almost came true."

For the ecstasy of his triumph in 1977, Watson had now suffered two losses at Turnberry which rank up there with some of the greatest disappointments of his career. In 1994 he started the final round one off the lead but slipped quietly down the leaderboard without making a challenge. That was not the case here and, as on Saturday, while others made their run, and their errors, Watson kept fighting to the point when he marched down the 18th fairway to the acclaim

Chris Wood tied for the lead on the 17th.

of the gallery with victory within sight.

Fourth Round Leaders

HOLE	1	2	3	4	5	6	7	8	9	10	11	12	13	14	15	16	17	18	
PAR	4	4	4	3	4	3	5	4	4	4	3	4	4	4	3	4	5	4	TOTAL
Stewart Cink	4	4	4	3	[5]	3	(4)	4	4	[5]	(2)	4	(3)	[5]	(2)	[5]	5	(3)	69-278
					4	3											(4)	(3)	14
Tom Watson	[5]	4	[5]	3	4	3	(4)	4	[5]	4	(2)	4	4	[5]	3	4	(4)	[5]	72-278
					[5]	3											[7]	[5]	20
Chris Wood	4	4	4	3	4	3	(3)	(3)	4	(3)	3	4	[5]	[5]	(2)	4	(4)	[5]	67-279
Lee Westwood	4	4	4	3	[5]	(2)	(3)	4	4	[5]	3	4	4	4	[4]	[5]	(4)	[5]	71-279
Luke Donald	(3)	4	4	(2)	4	3	5	[5]	4	(3)	3	4	4	[5]	(2)	4	(4)	4	67-280
Retief Goosen	4	[5]	4	3	4	3	5	4	4	4	3	[5]	4	4	[5]	4	(3)	4	72-280
Mathew Goggin	4	[5]	4	[4]	4	3	(4)	4	4	(3)	3	4	4	[5]	[4]	[5]	5	4	73-280
Soren Hansen	4	4	4	3	4	3	(4)	[5]	4	(3)	(2)	4	4	4	3	4	(4)	4	67-281
Justin Leonard	4	4	4	3	4	3	6	(3)	(3)	4	(2)	[5]	4	(3)	(2)	6	(4)	4	68-281
Ernie Els	(3)	4	4	3	4	3	(4)	4	4	(3)	3	[5]	(3)	4	3	[5]	(4)	[5]	68-281
Thomas Aiken	4	4	4	(2)	[5]	3	5	[5]	4	(3)	3	4	(3)	4	3	(3)	6	4	69-281
Richard S Johnson	4	4	[6]	3	4	(2)	(4)	[5]	(3)	(3)	3	4	4	[6]	(2)	[5]	(4)	4	70-281

Doing the same walk an hour later was even more emotional, the reception from the crowd even more heartfelt. "The memories are hard to forget," he said. "Coming up in the amphitheatre of the crowd and have them cheer you on like they do here for me. As I've said before, the feeling is mutual but that warmth makes you feel human. It makes you feel so good. I'll take those memories from this week and a sense of spirituality. There was something out there helping me along. I still believe that. It's Turnberry."

Cink, at 6ft 4in a gentle giant rather than an ogre, also received a generous ovation when he removed his cap to salute the crowd, smiled and accepted The Claret Jug with such evident joy. "I'm just filled with pride and honour," he said. "Having outlasted the field on this golf course with the way the weather beat us down the last three days, it's something I'll never forget. It's great to be the one left.

"And to play against Tom Watson in the playoff, it was mixed emotions, to be honest. I have watched him with such admiration this week. And going

Stewart Cink holed a 16-foot birdie putt on the 18th.

Excerpts FROM THE Press

Amateur Matteo Manassero finished on 69 and tied for 13th place.

way back, I could never have dreamed of going head-to-head against Tom Watson in a playoff for a Major championship. That would be beyond even my mind's imaginative capabilities. But then after playing with him in practice at the Masters this year, I would have told you I really don't ever want to have to go head-to-head against him because he hits it so well. The same Tom Watson that won this tournament in 1977 showed up here this week and he just about did it. He beat everybody but one guy. And it was really special."

Of course, Cink won partly because he was not wrapped up in the Watson nostalgia like the rest of us. So his was a different perspective, "engulfed by the joy," as he was. "I can understand the mystique that came really close to developing here," he added. "But in the end it's a tournament to see who lasts the longest. It's a survival test out there, as you can see by the winning score being two under. I'm pleased as punch I won this tournament and I'm also proud of the way Tom Watson played, because he showed not only what a great golfer he is but what a great game we all play, the longevity that can exist. We thought Jack Nicklaus had hung the moon when he won the Masters at 46. This was 13 years on. It says a lot about golf."

To complete the generational picture, also at the prize-giving was

Round Four Hole Summary

HOLE	PAR	YARDS	EAGLES	BIRDIES	PARS	BOGEYS	D.BOGEYS	HIGHER	RANK	AVERAGE
1	4	354	0	9	51	12	1	0	12	4.07
2	4	428	0	6	50	16	1	0	10	4.16
3	4	489	0	6	48	15	3	1	6	4.25
4	3	166	0	9	61	3	0	0	16	2.92
5	4	474	1	1	45	23	2	1	2	4.38
6	3	231	0	4	48	21	0	0	7	3.23
7	5	538	4	41	21	6	1	0	18	4.43
8	4	454	0	8	41	19	5	0	5	4.29
9	4	449	0	10	53	10	0	0	13	4.00
OUT	**35**	**3,583**	**5**	**94**	**418**	**125**	**13**	**2**		**35.73**
10	4	456	0	16	42	14	1	0	13	4.00
11	3	175	0	9	57	7	0	0	15	2.97
12	4	451	0	8	38	25	1	1	4	4.30
13	4	410	0	8	48	14	1	2	9	4.19
14	4	448	0	5	39	27	1	1	1	4.40
15	3	206	1	15	32	22	3	0	11	3.15
16	4	455	0	6	41	21	3	2	2	4.38
17	5	559	4	33	27	8	1	0	17	4.58
18	4	461	0	6	46	19	2	0	7	4.23
IN	**35**	**3,621**	**5**	**106**	**370**	**157**	**13**	**6**		**36.21**
TOTAL	**70**	**7,204**	**10**	**200**	**788**	**282**	**26**	**8**		**71.93**

Italy's Matteo Manassero, who at 16 was not only the youngest competitor in modern times but the youngest ever winner of the Silver Medal as the leading amateur in the 60 years since it has been awarded. Manassero was the only amateur to make the cut, but on the final day was only a few shots off the lead on the back nine before settling for a 69 and a tie for 13th place at two over-par. He said he would not be turning professional until after he had finished school, but if he needed any more inspiration after playing with the likes of Watson and Sergio Garcia during the week, it was the sight of the 2008 Silver Medallist, Wood, coming back the following year and contending for the title.

First, though, it was Ross Fisher who took the early spotlight. At the first he holed from 18 feet for a birdie and at the next he chipped in for another. What was the hurry? Was the baby on the way?

His 67 enabled Luke Donald to move from tied 27th to fifth.

Paul Lawrie went out in 31, including his albatross-2 on the seventh hole. He finished on 68.

It's a Fact

The albatross by Paul Lawrie — his 2 on the par-5 seventh hole in the fourth round — was the sixth albatross in The Open Championship since 1982. Lawrie holed out with a 4-iron from 213 yards. Others since 1982 were by Bill Rogers in 1983 at Royal Birkdale (hole 17, first round), Manny Zerman in 2000 at St Andrews (hole five, second round), Jeff Maggert (hole six, first round) and Greg Owen (hole 11, third round) in 2001 at Royal Lytham & St Annes, and Gary Evans at Royal Troon in 2004 (hole four, first round).

With Watson dropping a shot at the first, missing the green with a 6-iron, chipping then taking two putts from 10 feet, Fisher now led The Open by two strokes.

With the wind having shifted again, the front nine was playing more downwind and, while the back nine was proving tougher than the previous two days, Turnberry was also showing its ability to give with one hole and take with another. Paul Lawrie achieved his first ever albatross, and the first in The Open since Gary Evans at Royal Troon in 2004, by holing a 4-iron from 213 yards at the seventh. Five holes later the former Champion suffered a triple-bogey. American Kevin Sutherland also holed out from the fairway for an eagle-2 at the fifth but later had a 9 at the par-4 14th, which was rapidly turning into the hardest hole on the course. France's Thomas Levet, however, suffered no major reprisals for making a hole-in-one with a 5-iron at the 206-yard 15th hole.

Fisher missed the green on the right of the fourth and dropped a shot, but with Watson making a bogey at the third, missing the

Retief Goosen did not score a birdie until the 17th and finished on 72, tied for fifth.

Justin Leonard tied for eighth on 281.

Jeff Overton's 67 shared the low round.

Mathew Goggin tied for the lead, then fell back to tie for fifth with his 73.

Ross Fisher led by two strokes at the fifth hole, where he took an 8, a quadruple-bogey. This was his sixth shot.

Low Scores

Low First Nine	
Paul Lawrie	31
Low Second Nine	
Soren Hansen	32
Low Round	
Chris Wood	67
Luke Donald	67
Soren Hansen	67
Jeff Overton	67
Andres Romero	67

green again, this time with a 5-iron, Fisher was still two strokes clear. Until his disaster at the fifth. His drive also went right but he barely moved the ball with his second. His third, still from the rough, went over the fairway and now things were going from bad to worse. He had to take an unplayable and eventually holed out for an 8, a quadruple-bogey. Two more bogeys followed at the seventh and eighth holes, and although he finished with 10 straight pars for a 75, the Wentworth man was out of the picture at two-over 282. "It's a shame but I fought all the way," he said. "It was just one bad swing on the fifth. It's been a great week and I'm just glad I was here for the four days. Fingers crossed, in a couple of days I'll become a dad."

With Fisher falling away, the lead was now inherited by Watson and Wood. The 21-year-old from Bristol, in his rookie season on the European Tour, had returned rounds of 70, 70 and 72 and was now going superbly. He eagled the seventh from 12 feet and birdied the ninth from 10 feet to get under par for the Championship and holed from 25 feet for a 3 at the 10th. A chance went a begging at the 11th, but as he walked off the 12th green he was suddenly tied

An eagle-3 here at the seventh hole put Lee Westwood ahead by two strokes.

for the lead, although he was not sure of this because his caddie had instructed him not to look at the leaderboards.

Wood promptly dropped shots at the 13th and 14th holes and it was now Westwood who made his charge. Playing alongside Fisher, Westwood took over the baton, and although he had bogeyed the fifth while Fisher was having his troubles, he then holed from 20 feet for a 2 at the sixth and hit a beautiful 3-iron to 15 feet at the seventh and holed that for eagle-3. Now Westwood was ahead by two, although Watson got a birdie at the seventh, after reaching the green in two with a 2-hybrid club, to be only one behind until he bogeyed the ninth, where he hit a wedge short of the green.

Out in 33, Westwood drove into the rough at the 10th and took a

Soren Hansen's 67 took him from a tie for 40th to eighth.

Third in 2007, Andres Romero posted a 67 to tie for 13th.

5. When Watson's playing partner, Mathew Goggin, had a 3 at the hole moments later, Westwood and Goggin were now tied at three under. At the short 11th Watson holed another of his long putts, from 40 feet, and now there was a three-way tie.

Up ahead, Wood had recovered his composure and soon also his dropped shots. A 7-iron to 12 feet at the 15th gave him a 2, and he made a 4 at the 17th to get back to two under and one off the lead. At the last he had 210 yards to the hole and took a 9-iron, but the ball bounded on through the green. "I've never hit a 9-iron that far in my life," Wood said. "It was probably a little bit of adrenaline and a little bit of a flier from the semi-rough, you couldn't do anything about it. I hit a good shot, it landed exactly on the line I wanted, and it just went absolutely miles."

Wood was faced with a chip from the rough at the back of the green, and although he fancied get-

Chris Wood
From Fifth Place to Third to What's Next?

For some talented young amateur golfers, the hype surrounding their careers can raise the bar too high for comfort. And, for others, the lack of fanfare can allow the prodigy to fulfill their promise when they turn professional. In the case of Chris Wood, who came in under the radar at both Royal Birkdale and Turnberry, such an alluring gift for the linksland game is unlikely to escape the glare of media attention when he tees-up in the future.

Still only 21 and making a decent fist of his rookie season on the European Tour, Wood pulled off the remarkable feat on the Ailsa course of improving on his share of fifth place in Southport a year earlier by finishing in a tie for third with Lee Westwood in Ayrshire. Amazingly, had he not overcooked a 9-iron and dropped a shot on the 72nd hole, the former youth centre-forward with Bristol City would have been involved in the four-hole playoff with Tom Watson and Stewart Cink.

Two Opens, two top-five finishes, and yet when Wood missed the 18th green through the back and failed to get up and down for par, he was torn between pride in producing another outstanding performance and frustration at not accomplishing even more. After watching Cink set the mark, the young Englishman got into his automobile and drove for seven hours to sleep in his own bed in Bristol. "It was only the next morning it really hit me," he recalled. "And it's gutting. It occurred to me I had a real chance to win The Open, and came up just short."

With a similar lanky build to the towering England striker Peter Crouch, Wood was once tipped for the big time in soccer before a serious knee injury curtailed his involvement with the game. Football's loss was golf's gain, and the tall, slim lad with spiky hair struck a blow for the emerging generation in a Championship where most of the contenders were in their 30s, 40s and 50s.

Tipping 6ft 5in with a trim physique, you'd expect Wood to be buffeted like a flagstick on a breezy links. Not a bit of it. He was so secure in his own ability that in spite of starting the last round on two over-par, six shots off the lead, Wood hunted down the more fancied names and, thanks to an eagle at the seventh, posted a 67 for an aggregate of 279.

Glad to subsidise the purchase of a new flat with a cheque for £255,000 — his amateur status meant he'd missed out on more than £168,000 a year earlier — Wood also knew the value of his experiences in The Open were immeasurable. "It's weird to say I'm only 21 and I've contended in two Majors already," he said. "The experiences I've got out of The Open are going to be amazing for my career. I'm just going to move on every year."

—Mike Aitken

After hitting a 9-iron a massive 210 yards through the 18th green, Chris Wood chipped 20 feet short of the hole and took a bogey.

Excerpts FROM THE Press

"The view from the 10th at Turnberry is as good as it gets in golf. Chris Wood's mother Sara called it 'spectacular.' But it was not the lighthouse, Ailsa Craig or Irish Sea lapping the rocky shore of Ayshire's beautiful coast. It was the sight of her son's name at the top of The Open leaderboard."

—**Matthew Dunn**, *Daily Express*

"Stewart Cink's caddie knew the real significance of his boss' Open victory Sunday. It goes back eight years, back to when Cink gave away a chance to win the 2001 US Open on the 18th green at Southern Hills in Tulsa. Now he can finally let that go. 'He needed it,' Frank Williams said."

—**Hank Gola**, *New York Daily News*

"Sergio Garcia made it 41 Majors without a victory when he came home with a one-over 71 at Turnberry. The 29-year-old Spaniard, who was one under at the halfway stage of the tournament, had slipped back with a third-round six-over-par 76."

—**Robert Millwood**, *The Scotsman*

"Tom Watson stood over an eight-foot par putt on the final hole of a mystical Open, one stroke away from becoming the oldest Major champion in history. For the first time all week, he showed his 59-year-old nerves. The putt never had a chance. A little more than an hour later, neither did Watson."

—**Doug Ferguson**, *The Associated Press*

In his stop-start round, Cink hit his second shot to the fifth hole into a bunker.

ting the ball close, it ran 20 feet past and he took a 5. It was a 67 and now he was the leader in the clubhouse at one-under 279. Only later would it become obvious that a par at the last would have got the youngster in the playoff — something he had to contemplate on the long drive south — but at that time it looked like a highly creditable follow-up to finishing fifth as an amateur the year before. "To follow up on last year as a professional is great, this is a better performance," he said. "It's weird to say I'm only 21 and I've contended in two Majors already. My experiences at The Open already have been amazing. It was ironic playing with Justin Rose today, we've both made our names at The Open."

With an 8-iron downwind to six feet for a birdie at the 15th hole, Cink got within one of the lead for the third time during the afternoon. His had been a stop-start final round. He bogeyed the fifth but birdied the seventh to get back to one under, at which point he was just one back and the closest he had been to the lead since he bogeyed the 18th on Thursday to drop behind Watson's early clubhouse lead. He bogeyed the 10th but got that shot back with a 25-foot putt for a 2 at the 11th. Then he got to two under with an 18-foot putt for a 3 at the 13th, one off the lead again. The pattern

Ernie Els climbed to a tie for eighth, finishing on 68 and a 281 aggregate.

Miguel Angel Jimenez finished on 69 to tie for 13th.

Justin Rose's 70 placed him in a tie for 13th.

Thomas Aiken posted a 69 to be on 281.

After hitting into a fairway bunker at the 10th, Cink reached the green in three and took two putts for a bogey.

Fourth Round Scores	
Players Under Par	16
Players At Par	11
Players Over Par	46

continued as he flared a 5-iron to the right and bogeyed the 14th before claiming another 2, this time at the short 15th.

The rollercoaster continued, and three putts from 45 feet for a bogey at the 16th dropped him two behind Westwood, who now led on his own as Watson and Goggin bogeyed the 14th. The Australian bogeyed three of the last five holes and drifted out of the picture, but now Westwood had his best ever chance of winning a Major. What he did not want to do was bogey three of the last four holes. At the 15th, his tee shot almost hit the flagstick but bounded on into the back bunker. He could not get up and down, and nor could he at the next when his approach went over the green. Watson, who had bogeyed the 14th after hitting short of the green with a 2-hybrid, parred the 15th and 16th and was back in the lead on his own for the first time since teeing off.

Cink was still remarkably calm, even though he could not birdie the 17th, missing a putt from eight feet. "I never felt nervous at all," Cink said. "I just felt so calm in a situation where in the past I would be extremely nervous. I felt totally at peace with whatever happened. I'm not sure I really thought much about whether I was

Round of the **Day**

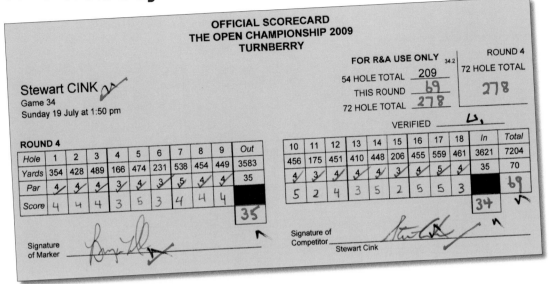

OFFICIAL SCORECARD
THE OPEN CHAMPIONSHIP 2009
TURNBERRY

FOR R&A USE ONLY 34.2

ROUND 4
72 HOLE TOTAL

54 HOLE TOTAL _209_
THIS ROUND _69_
72 HOLE TOTAL _278_

_278_

Stewart CINK
Game 34
Sunday 19 July at 1:50 pm

VERIFIED _____

ROUND 4

Hole	1	2	3	4	5	6	7	8	9	Out
Yards	354	428	489	166	474	231	538	454	449	3583
Par	4	4	4	3	4	3	5	4	4	35
Score	4	4	4	3	5	3	4	4	4	35

10	11	12	13	14	15	16	17	18	In	Total
456	175	451	410	448	206	455	559	461	3621	7204
4	3	4	4	4	3	4	5	4	35	70
5	2	4	3	5	2	5	5	3	34	69

Signature
of Marker

Signature of
Competitor _Stewart Cink_

Stewart Cink made only two pars in his last nine holes while posting a 69, and one of those came on a missed eight-foot birdie putt on the 17th which at the time seemed to have dimmed his hopes.

Cink went out in level-par 35 with a bogey on the fifth and a birdie on the seventh. He drove into the rough on the fifth, hit his second into a bunker, and came out to 20 feet. He reached the green at the seventh with a drive and 3-wood and just missed a 40-foot eagle putt.

He bogeyed the 10th when his 4-iron tee shot rolled into a fairway bunker and he had to pitch out. After a third shot he had two putts from 15 feet. A birdie on the short 11th came on a wedge shot and a 25-foot putt. A 5-iron off the 13th tee and a wedge to 18 feet resulted in a birdie there. He bogeyed the 14th after a perfect drive, when his 5-iron approach flared 25 yards to the right.

Cink's 8-iron shot to six feet produced a birdie on the 15th, but then he was short of the green on the 16th and had a three-putt bogey from 45 feet.

After a 2-iron off the 18th tee, Cink debated whether to use an 8 or 9-iron next. Certain that an 8-iron shot would be over the green, Cink played short with a 9-iron, and his shot rolled pin-high, 16 feet from the hole, producing the birdie that secured his playoff spot.

Watson bogeyed here on the 14th, and Westwood led at three under.

Westwood sent his 45-foot putt on the 18th six feet past, and missed the par-saver.

good enough to win a Major or not. I knew I had been close a few times but I never heard my name tossed in there with the group of the best ones not to have won. So maybe I was starting to believe that I wasn't one of the best ones never to have won a Major. But this week for some reason I just believed I had something good going. Somebody at a Major championship always has that calm peace about them and I had it today."

A 2-iron off the 18th tee left him in the fairway with 190 yards to the green, and Cink debated whether to use an 8 or 9-iron next. It was a decision that Watson behind him would soon also consider. Certain that an 8-iron shot would be over the green, Cink played short with a 9-iron, and his judgment was proven correct as his shot rolled pin-high, 16 feet from the hole. "I don't remember know-

Westwood's Regret
Feeling sick after taking three putts to miss the playoff

For every person who dwelt on how Lee Westwood came up short in the 2009 Open, there would have been another who would have left Turnberry doubly convinced that the Englishman's time will come before too long.

Just take the way he played over the first two rounds in the company of Tiger Woods and the 17-year-old Ryo Ishikawa. Not too long ago, Westwood would have been distracted by the hoards of cameramen attached to his playing companions. As it was, he coped admirably, keeping his focus at all times in opening with a 68 and a 70 for a halfway tally of 138.

It is one thing to be paired with Woods when he is playing well, as he mostly was in his opening 71. Quite another to be partnering the world number one when he was embroiled in the kind of mid-round nightmare he had on the Friday as he dropped six shots in the space of seven holes on his way to a 75 and a missed cut.

The latter was a different experience for Westwood, but it was typical of how he is today that he had the confidence not to feel awkward in any way. "I was in my own little world," he said afterwards.

Westwood's second-round 70 was, in fact, a mature effort in every sense. "I didn't squander shots," he said, in a reference to the mischievously buffeting wind. "It was very much a case of trying to keep grinding out the pars until I got to the back nine and a few of the downwind holes." As it was, he birdied the 15th and the 17th.

Westwood said that his aim over the weekend was to keep doing what he had been doing and he stuck rigidly to that plan.

After a third round taking in nothing more erratic than two bogeys and two birdies, Westwood, like Goosen, was two shots behind Tom Watson and one behind Mathew Goggin and Ross Fisher. Things changed, rapidly, as Fisher leapt two ahead of all four of Watson, Goggin, Wood and Westwood in the space of the first four holes. And they changed again when it came to the fifth. Fisher and Westwood hit much the same tee shots into the grassy bank on the right before things went from bad to worse for Fisher — he amassed an 8 — as Westwood escaped with a bogey.

Though Fisher continued to struggle thereafter, Westwood put his minor hiccup behind him as he went birdie, eagle at the sixth and seventh to be the man at the top of the leaderboard. From that point, he led or vied for the lead all afternoon before making bogeys on three of the last four holes for the 71 which left him one shot away from joining the playoff.

It was the three putts on the 18th he would rue the most. "I've gone from frustration to sickness now," he said, minutes after he had watched on a television monitor as Watson bogeyed the 72nd to lose his lead. "I played great all week. Third place is not to be sniffed at in a Major championship, but I'm disappointed, really."

Amid that disappointment, he was almost unfairly tough on himself, saying: "I've had my share of disasters in golf — and mainly when it mattered most."

—**Lewine Mair**

---

ing exactly what I needed to do, but I just knew I wanted to try and make that putt," Cink said. "I've been working really hard on my putting and my mental approach and this was another test. I had a good solid routine going and I hit that putt without a care in the world of whether it went in or it missed. A blank mind like that is the best way to approach a pressure-packed situation and I was proud of the way I handled that."

Cink was the new clubhouse leader at 278, two under-par after a 69, and for the first time in the afternoon he was tied for the lead with Watson out on the course. Westwood joined them with a birdie at the 17th after an exquisite 5-iron finished 15 feet short of the hole. His eagle attempt very

Two putts from the fringe at 17 gave Watson a birdie.

Watson hit through the green with his 8-iron, then putted eight feet past and missed his chance at a sixth Open title.

Previous pages, Cink holed for a birdie on the 18th from 16 feet after reaching the green with a 9-iron shot.

nearly dropped, and how different things might have been had it done so.

Following up behind, Watson also birdied the 17th, reaching the fringe in two with a 2-hybrid, to go back in front by one. Worse for Westwood, his drive at the last ran into one of the bunkers guarding the corner of the dogleg. With fortunes shifting by the minute, Westwood restored his hopes by effecting a miraculous recovery with a 9-iron that found the green. He was a long way away, 45 feet from the hole, but a 4 was still a possibility. Yet, looking behind him, Westwood saw Watson's drive split the fairway.

Westwood's game plan changed again. "I thought I had to hole that putt, to be perfectly honest," he admitted. "I didn't see Tom bogeying the last from the fairway, since he's such an experienced player. I shouldn't have got ahead of myself." Westwood ran the putt past by six feet and could not hole the par-saver. After a 71 he was back at one-under

Championship Hole Summary

HOLE	PAR	YARDS	EAGLES	BIRDIES	PARS	BOGEYS	D.BOGEYS	HIGHER	RANK	AVERAGE
1	4	354	0	71	308	75	3	1	15	4.03
2	4	428	0	27	308	113	8	2	9	4.24
3	4	489	0	36	312	101	7	2	11	4.19
4	3	166	0	60	331	57	8	2	14	3.04
5	4	474	1	30	224	171	29	3	1	4.45
6	3	231	0	27	304	113	13	1	8	3.25
7	5	538	18	184	201	45	9	1	17	4.66
8	4	454	0	34	260	141	22	1	2	4.34
9	4	449	0	39	271	134	13	1	6	4.27
OUT	35	3,583	19	508	2,519	950	112	14		36.48
10	4	456	0	50	268	111	23	6	5	4.28
11	3	175	0	48	361	46	2	1	16	3.01
12	4	451	0	45	272	117	21	3	7	4.27
13	4	410	0	57	302	79	15	4	13	4.14
14	4	448	0	35	269	132	20	1	3	4.31
15	3	206	1	53	293	87	21	2	12	3.18
16	4	455	0	53	278	78	39	9	4	4.29
17	5	559	21	246	157	28	4	1	18	4.46
18	4	461	0	49	279	113	14	2	10	4.21
IN	35	3,621	22	636	2,479	791	159	29		36.14
TOTAL	70	7,204	41	1144	4,998	1,741	271	43		72.62

279, level with Wood and one behind Cink and two behind Watson. When it turned out his final bogey had meant he missed out on the playoff, he admitted: "I've gone from frustration to sickness now. I played great all week. Third place is not to be sniffed at in a Major championship, but I'm disappointed, really." With a series of junior clinics arranged for the following week, Westwood would have been able to show off the real Claret Jug to the youngsters.

In the middle of the 18th fairway 32 years ago, Alfie Fyles, Watson's famous Open-winning caddie, advised taking a 7-iron rather than a 6 and Watson put his approach to two feet. Now Watson considered a 9-iron but went with an 8 — the opposite of Cink's choice. He hit the shot as he intended but the ball took a hard bounce and wouldn't stop on the green. "That 8-iron will always live with me," he said. "I hit the shot I wanted to hit and it had the whole length of the green to stop and it never did." He had an awkward lie just off the fringe and decided to putt, but the ball ran eight feet past. "I thought it might be a little slow and just gave it a bit too much goose," he said. Standing over the putt, for par and victory, was suddenly an old Tom Watson, not the Tom Watson of old. It was short and right and did not deserve to win any championship, leaving him

Championship Totals	
Rounds Under Par	78
Rounds At Par	50
Rounds Over Par	329

4

The four-hole playoff journey began here on the fifth hole, then went to the sixth, 17th and 18th holes.

with a 72 and tied with Cink at 278. Suddenly, he was gone. There was nothing left.

Starting the playoff at the fifth, both players were bunkered in two, but after that Cink did not put a foot wrong. He got up and down to go one ahead, and then at the sixth Watson's tee shot scattered the crowd on the right. He made a par but across at the 17th he hooked his drive and took two more to escape the hay. A double-bogey handed Cink a four-shot advantage and Watson's face on the 18th tee was heartbreakingly mournful. "The playoff was just one bad shot after another," he said. "I didn't give Stewart much competition. It looked like I ran out of gas, didn't it, but I didn't feel that. I hit a chubby 5-iron for my second at the fifth, I got stuck on the hybrid on the sixth, and my legs didn't work on the drive on the 17th. By that time Stewart had it pretty well in hand."

Watson summed up the mood in his press conference with his opening words: "This ain't a funeral, you know." He was, as ever, gracious in defeat. One of the first people to contact to him that night was Nicklaus. "He was very upset, and he should have been very upset," Nicklaus revealed in an interview for *Sports Illustrated*

Cink saved par on the first playoff hole to lead by one.

Watson drove in the rough on the third playoff hole, taking 7 to Cink's 4.

"One of golf's truly great guys turned out to be the bad guy. Even Stewart Cink recognised that in the gathering darkness Sunday night at Turnberry, where you could hear a Claret Jug drop."

—**Bob Harig, ESPN.com**

"The Claret Jug is back on Padraig Harrington's breakfast table, just as it has been for the past two years. The Irishman didn't have the heart to tell his two young kids that he hadn't won it again. So he sneaked on a replica instead."

—**Derek Lawrenson, *Daily Mail***

"Reporters from all over the world, several of whom had been at Carnoustie to cover Tom Watson's first Open Championship victory 34 years ago, filed sombrely into the interview room, where he waited patiently, and took their seats. Finally, Watson could stand it no longer. 'This ain't a funeral, you know,' he said with a sad and weary smile."

—**Helen Ross, PGATour.com**

"A little bit of magic perished in the gloaming Sunday at Turnberry. Stewart Cink by six strokes in a four-hole play-off over Tom Watson simply wasn't the way it was supposed to end. Tom Watson deserved better. … Stewart Cink deserved better."

—**Barker Davis,
*The Washington Times***

Caddie Frank
Williams offered
Cink his con-
gratulations on
the final hole.

Caddie Frank Williams offered Cink his congratulations on the final hole.

magazine. "I would have been very upset, and I was very upset for him. It was obvious when he got to the playoff that he had spent all his emotion and energy and didn't have much left.

"Tom has not lost his ability to swing the golf club. He drove it exceptionally straight. British seaside golf courses don't require length, so he wasn't stressed out as far as having to drive the ball a long distance. He managed his game well. He just didn't make the last putt. Win or lose, he ended up doing something unbelievable, and we were all really proud of him. It was a great effort, and it makes us old folks feel good."

While Watson hacked his way to a final bogey, Cink, after a birdie at the 17th, finished the playoff in style by hitting a wedge to four feet and holing that for a 3. "It doesn't get any more satisfying than this," he said. "After all the changes I've made, with The Claret Jug in my hands I guess this transformation is complete. The journey is not over but I'm a believer now."

There would be much celebrating and tweeting to come. Two messages stuck out. In one Cink described how a friend had placed a bet on him of $40 at 125 to 1. "He bets on me every Major. Says he's now just above break-even." Another said simply: "Not sure what to say but this picture should do the trick...." It was of Cink kissing The Claret Jug. And why not? It's got his name on it.

Let Us Cheer for Cink and His Victory

By John Hopkins

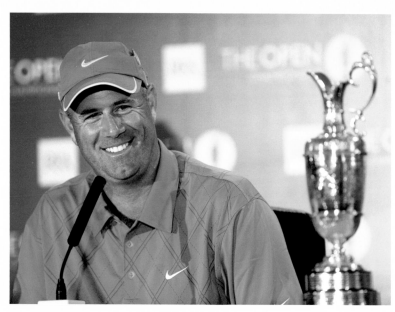

Question: When all the hullabaloo had died down, who was it who held up the old trophy? Who played the four playoff holes in fewer strokes than his rival. Who birdied the 72nd hole to set a clubhouse target?

It wasn't Tom Watson. It wasn't the 59-year-old man with the nine-month-old left hip we had all wanted to win. He wouldn't be cradling the trophy having won it for a record-equalling sixth time 34 years after he had won it for the first time.

It was, instead, Stewart Cink, and before we rush to rain even more plaudits on the head of Watson, let us not forget why Cink won. He won because he had done his apprenticeship as a professional golfer and learned from it.

He took something out of being beaten 8 & 7 by Tiger Woods in the final of the 2008 Accenture Match Play Championship. He won five times on the US Tour, twice at Hilton Head and twice at Hartford, each second victory demonstrating what he had learned from his first.

Those tournament successes in the US had helped forge a competitive nature that was not immediately obvious to someone looking upon a tall, gawky almost, man of 6ft 4in, with little hair and a slow friendly smile, a man who Twitters as if there is no tomorrow. Cink looks a nice man and is a nice man. What he demonstrated at Turnberry was that now, at 36 and after 14 years as a professional, he was competitively sharp enough and mentally resilient enough to triumph when given the chance.

The winner of an event like this often speaks afterwards of things such as fate and the rub of the green. After some of his victories, Severiano Ballesteros used to say: "It was destino" or "I was destined to win." Just before the 1987 Open at Muirfield Nick Faldo dreamed of seeing his name on top of the leaderboard. He thought to himself: "I can handle that." He did not have any feelings of diffidence or inferiority, so it was no real surprise when he became The Open Champion the following Sunday.

For Turnberry, Cink was as prepared as he ever had been. Seven days spent playing golf in Ireland at Ballybunion, Lahinch and Doonbeg while staying at Doonbeg had reminded him of the rhythms, rituals and mental disciplines that are essential for a golfer to be able to compete on links courses. "I shot high scores, made some big numbers on some holes," Cink said. "I came to Turnberry, you would think, maybe a little frustrated or questionable … but no, I came here knowing that, hey, this is what you get when you play links golf. I was ready to go."

And then he discovered something else that made him think it might, after all, be his time. "There is always a person who feels an inner calm the week of a Major championship," Cink said. "This week I was that man. I did not feel nervous in situations where I have felt nervous in the past."

Yet even in victory Cink seemed to be the loser. Instead of hailing him, everyone lauded Watson. In its edition of Monday 20 July, *The Times* carried a front-page photograph of Watson and an editorial was devoted to him. "Before his heroism this week Watson was a master," the newspaper said. "Now he is a legend."

Cink was like the man who had shot Bambi, who had killed Santa Claus. He had spoiled arguably the greatest golf story ever, better even than Ouimet in 1913, Hogan in 1953 and Woods' 15-stroke victory in the 2000 US Open. Cink's victory was the only known case of a man of 6ft 4in being overshadowed by a man of 5ft 9in.

But Cink had that worked out, too. He understood how his finest victory was dwarfed by a greater story and he demonstrated no peevishness at what many might have seen as a lack of appreciation of his efforts.

"I knew what to expect," he said later. "I played with Lee (Westwood) on Saturday and the crowds cheered for him, quite rightly. I am often the guy who the crowds respect but are not 100 percent behind."

So let us cheer for Cink and his first victory in a Major championship even if we weep for Watson at what might have been.

In a country that saw the birth of the game and one year after a man only six years younger had played such a powerful role in the ultimate triumph by Padraig Harrington, Cink's victory in The Open was nothing less than a rebirth of golf as a game for all ages. Oh yes, and it was a helluva Championship.

The Open Championship Results

Year	Champion	Score	Margin	Runners-up	Venue
1860	Willie Park Snr	174	2	Tom Morris Snr	Prestwick
1861	Tom Morris Snr	163	4	Willie Park Snr	Prestwick
1862	Tom Morris Snr	163	13	Willie Park Snr	Prestwick
1863	Willie Park Snr	168	2	Tom Morris Snr	Prestwick
1864	Tom Morris Snr	167	2	Andrew Strath	Prestwick
1865	Andrew Strath	162	2	Willie Park Snr	Prestwick
1866	Willie Park Snr	169	2	David Park	Prestwick
1867	Tom Morris Snr	170	2	Willie Park Snr	Prestwick
1868	Tom Morris Jnr	154	3	Tom Morris Snr	Prestwick
1869	Tom Morris Jnr	157	11	Bob Kirk	Prestwick
1870	Tom Morris Jnr	149	12	Bob Kirk, David Strath	Prestwick
1871	*No Competition*				
1872	Tom Morris Jnr	166	3	David Strath	Prestwick
1873	Tom Kidd	179	1	Jamie Anderson	St Andrews
1874	Mungo Park	159	2	Tom Morris Jnr	Musselburgh
1875	Willie Park Snr	166	2	Bob Martin	Prestwick
1876	Bob Martin	176	—	David Strath	St Andrews
	(Martin was awarded the title when Strath refused to play-off)				
1877	Jamie Anderson	160	2	Bob Pringle	Musselburgh
1878	Jamie Anderson	157	2	Bob Kirk	Prestwick
1879	Jamie Anderson	169	3	James Allan, Andrew Kirkaldy	St Andrews
1880	Bob Ferguson	162	5	Peter Paxton	Musselburgh
1881	Bob Ferguson	170	3	Jamie Anderson	Prestwick
1882	Bob Ferguson	171	3	Willie Fernie	St Andrews
1883	Willie Fernie	158	Playoff	Bob Ferguson	Musselburgh
1884	Jack Simpson	160	4	Douglas Rolland, Willie Fernie	Prestwick
1885	Bob Martin	171	1	Archie Simpson	St Andrews
1886	David Brown	157	2	Willie Campbell	Musselburgh
1887	Willie Park Jnr	161	1	Bob Martin	Prestwick
1888	Jack Burns	171	1	David Anderson Jnr, Ben Sayers	St Andrews
1889	Willie Park Jnr	155	Playoff	Andrew Kirkaldy	Musselburgh
1890	John Ball Jnr*	164	3	Willie Fernie, Archie Simpson	Prestwick
1891	Hugh Kirkaldy	166	2	Willie Fernie, Andrew Kirkaldy	St Andrews
	(From 1892 the competition was extended to 72 holes)				
1892	Harold Hilton*	305	3	John Ball Jnr*, Hugh Kirkaldy, Sandy Herd	Muirfield

Year	Champion	Score	Margin	Runners-up	Venue
1893	Willie Auchterlonie	322	2	John Laidlay*	Prestwick
1894	JH Taylor	326	5	Douglas Rolland	Royal St George's
1895	JH Taylor	322	4	Sandy Herd	St Andrews
1896	Harry Vardon	316	Playoff	JH Taylor	Muirfield
1897	Harold Hilton*	314	1	James Braid	Royal Liverpool
1898	Harry Vardon	307	1	Willie Park Jnr	Prestwick
1899	Harry Vardon	310	5	Jack White	Royal St George's
1900	JH Taylor	309	8	Harry Vardon	St Andrews
1901	James Braid	309	3	Harry Vardon	Muirfield
1902	Sandy Herd	307	1	Harry Vardon, James Braid	Royal Liverpool
1903	Harry Vardon	300	6	Tom Vardon	Prestwick
1904	Jack White	296	1	James Braid, JH Taylor	Royal St George's
1905	James Braid	318	5	JH Taylor, Rowland Jones	St Andrews
1906	James Braid	300	4	JH Taylor	Muirfield
1907	Arnaud Massy	312	2	JH Taylor	Royal Liverpool
1908	James Braid	291	8	Tom Ball	Prestwick
1909	JH Taylor	295	6	James Braid, Tom Ball	Deal
1910	James Braid	299	4	Sandy Herd	St Andrews
1911	Harry Vardon	303	Playoff	Arnaud Massy	Royal St George's
1912	Ted Ray	295	4	Harry Vardon	Muirfield
1913	JH Taylor	304	8	Ted Ray	Royal Liverpool
1914	Harry Vardon	306	3	JH Taylor	Prestwick
1915-1919	*No Championship*				
1920	George Duncan	303	2	Sandy Herd	Deal
1921	Jock Hutchison	296	Playoff	Roger Wethered*	St Andrews
1922	Walter Hagen	300	1	George Duncan, Jim Barnes	Royal St George's
1923	Arthur G. Havers	295	1	Walter Hagen	Troon
1924	Walter Hagen	301	1	Ernest Whitcombe	Royal Liverpool
1925	Jim Barnes	300	1	Archie Compston, Ted Ray	Prestwick
1926	Robert T. Jones Jnr*	291	2	Al Watrous	Royal Lytham
1927	Robert T. Jones Jnr*	285	6	Aubrey Boomer, Fred Robson	St Andrews
1928	Walter Hagen	292	2	Gene Sarazen	Royal St George's
1929	Walter Hagen	292	6	John Farrell	Muirfield

Tom Watson (1975, 1977, 1980, 1982, 1983)

Sandy Lyle (1985)

Mark Calcavecchia (1989)

Tiger Woods (2000, 2005, 2006)

Greg Norman (1986, 1993)

Year	Champion	Score	Margin	Runners-up	Venue
1930	Robert T. Jones Jnr*	291	2	Leo Diegel, Macdonald Smith	Royal Liverpool
1931	Tommy Armour	296	1	Jose Jurado	Carnoustie
1932	Gene Sarazen	283	5	Macdonald Smith	Prince's
1933	Densmore Shute	292	Playoff	Craig Wood	St Andrews
1934	Henry Cotton	283	5	Sid Brews	Royal St George's
1935	Alf Perry	283	4	Alf Padgham	Muirfield
1936	Alf Padgham	287	1	Jimmy Adams	Royal Liverpool
1937	Henry Cotton	290	2	Reg Whitcombe	Carnoustie
1938	Reg Whitcombe	295	2	Jimmy Adams	Royal St George's
1939	Richard Burton	290	2	Johnny Bulla	St Andrews
1940-1945	*No Championship*				
1946	Sam Snead	290	4	Bobby Locke, Johnny Bulla	St Andrews
1947	Fred Daly	293	1	Reg Horne, Frank Stranahan*	Royal Liverpool
1948	Henry Cotton	284	5	Fred Daly	Muirfield
1949	Bobby Locke	283	Playoff	Harry Bradshaw	Royal St George's
1950	Bobby Locke	279	2	Roberto de Vicenzo	Troon
1951	Max Faulkner	285	2	Tony Cerda	Royal Portrush
1952	Bobby Locke	287	1	Peter Thomson	Royal Lytham
1953	Ben Hogan	282	4	Frank Stranahan*, Dai Rees, Peter Thomson, Tony Cerda	Carnoustie
1954	Peter Thomson	283	1	Sid Scott, Dai Rees, Bobby Locke	Royal Birkdale
1955	Peter Thomson	281	2	Johnny Fallon	St Andrews
1956	Peter Thomson	286	3	Flory van Donck	Royal Liverpool
1957	Bobby Locke	279	3	Peter Thomson	St Andrews
1958	Peter Thomson	278	Playoff	David Thomas	Royal Lytham
1959	Gary Player	284	2	Flory van Donck, Fred Bullock	Muirfield
1960	Kel Nagle	278	1	Arnold Palmer	St Andrews
1961	Arnold Palmer	284	1	Dai Rees	Royal Birkdale
1962	Arnold Palmer	276	6	Kel Nagle	Troon
1963	Bob Charles	277	Playoff	Phil Rodgers	Royal Lytham
1964	Tony Lema	279	5	Jack Nicklaus	St Andrews
1965	Peter Thomson	285	2	Christy O'Connor, Brian Huggett	Royal Birkdale
1966	Jack Nicklaus	282	1	David Thomas, Doug Sanders	Muirfield
1967	Roberto de Vicenzo	278	2	Jack Nicklaus	Royal Liverpool
1968	Gary Player	289	2	Jack Nicklaus, Bob Charles	Carnoustie
1969	Tony Jacklin	280	2	Bob Charles	Royal Lytham
1970	Jack Nicklaus	283	Playoff	Doug Sanders	St Andrews
1971	Lee Trevino	278	1	Lu Liang Huan	Royal Birkdale
1972	Lee Trevino	278	1	Jack Nicklaus	Muirfield
1973	Tom Weiskopf	276	3	Neil Coles, Johnny Miller	Troon
1974	Gary Player	282	4	Peter Oosterhuis	Royal Lytham

Year	Champion	Score	Margin	Runners-up	Venue
1975	Tom Watson	279	Playoff	Jack Newton	Carnoustie
1976	Johnny Miller	279	6	Jack Nicklaus, Severiano Ballesteros	Royal Birkdale
1977	Tom Watson	268	1	Jack Nicklaus	Turnberry
1978	Jack Nicklaus	281	2	Simon Owen, Ben Crenshaw, Raymond Floyd, Tom Kite	St Andrews
1979	Severiano Ballesteros	283	3	Jack Nicklaus, Ben Crenshaw	Royal Lytham
1980	Tom Watson	271	4	Lee Trevino	Muirfield
1981	Bill Rogers	276	4	Bernhard Langer	Royal St George's
1982	Tom Watson	284	1	Peter Oosterhuis, Nick Price	Royal Troon
1983	Tom Watson	275	1	Hale Irwin, Andy Bean	Royal Birkdale
1984	Severiano Ballesteros	276	2	Bernhard Langer, Tom Watson	St Andrews
1985	Sandy Lyle	282	1	Payne Stewart	Royal St George's
1986	Greg Norman	280	5	Gordon J. Brand	Turnberry
1987	Nick Faldo	279	1	Rodger Davis, Paul Azinger	Muirfield
1988	Severiano Ballesteros	273	2	Nick Price	Royal Lytham
1989	Mark Calcavecchia	275	Playoff	Greg Norman, Wayne Grady	Royal Troon
1990	Nick Faldo	270	5	Mark McNulty, Payne Stewart	St Andrews
1991	Ian Baker-Finch	272	2	Mike Harwood	Royal Birkdale
1992	Nick Faldo	272	1	John Cook	Muirfield
1993	Greg Norman	267	2	Nick Faldo	Royal St George's
1994	Nick Price	268	1	Jesper Parnevik	Turnberry
1995	John Daly	282	Playoff	Costantino Rocca	St Andrews
1996	Tom Lehman	271	2	Mark McCumber, Ernie Els	Royal Lytham
1997	Justin Leonard	272	3	Jesper Parnevik, Darren Clarke	Royal Troon
1998	Mark O'Meara	280	Playoff	Brian Watts	Royal Birkdale
1999	Paul Lawrie	290	Playoff	Justin Leonard, Jean Van de Velde	Carnoustie
2000	Tiger Woods	269	8	Ernie Els, Thomas Bjorn	St Andrews
2001	David Duval	274	3	Niclas Fasth	Royal Lytham
2002	Ernie Els	278	Playoff	Thomas Levet, Stuart Appleby, Steve Elkington	Muirfield
2003	Ben Curtis	283	1	Thomas Bjorn, Vijay Singh	Royal St George's
2004	Todd Hamilton	274	Playoff	Ernie Els	Royal Troon
2005	Tiger Woods	274	5	Colin Montgomerie	St Andrews
2006	Tiger Woods	270	2	Chris DiMarco	Royal Liverpool
2007	Padraig Harrington	277	Playoff	Sergio Garcia	Carnoustie
2008	Padraig Harrington	283	4	Ian Poulter	Royal Birkdale
2009	Stewart Cink	278	Playoff	Tom Watson	Turnberry

*Denotes amateurs

Sir Nick Faldo (1987, 1990, 1992)

Todd Hamilton (2004)

Ernie Els (2002)

The Open Championship Records

Most Victories

6, Harry Vardon, 1896-98-99-1903-11-14

5, James Braid, 1901-05-06-08-10; JH Taylor, 1894-95-1900-09-13; Peter Thomson, 1954-55-56-58-65; Tom Watson, 1975-77-80-82-83

Most Times Runner-Up or Joint Runner-Up

7, Jack Nicklaus, 1964-67-68-72-76-77-79

6, JH Taylor, 1896-1904-05-06-07-14

Oldest Winner

Old Tom Morris, 46 years 99 days, 1867

Roberto de Vicenzo, 44 years 93 days, 1967

Harry Vardon, 44 years 41 days, 1914

Youngest Winner

Young Tom Morris, 17 years 5 months 3 days, 1868

Willie Auchterlonie, 21 years 24 days, 1893

Severiano Ballesteros, 22 years 3 months 12 days, 1979

John Daly (1995)

Youngest and Oldest Competitor

Young Tom Morris, 14 years 4 months 25 days, 1865

Gene Sarazen, 74 years 4 months 9 days, 1976

Biggest Margin of Victory

13 strokes, Old Tom Morris, 1862

12 strokes, Young Tom Morris, 1870

11 strokes, Young Tom Morris, 1869

8 strokes, JH Taylor, 1900 and 1913; James Braid, 1908; Tiger Woods, 2000

Lowest Winning Aggregates

267 (66, 68, 69, 64), Greg Norman, Royal St George's, 1993

268 (68, 70, 65, 65), Tom Watson, Turnberry, 1977; (69, 66, 67, 66), Nick Price, Turnberry, 1994

269 (67, 66, 67, 69), Tiger Woods, St Andrews, 2000

Lowest Aggregates in Relation to Par

269 (19 under-par), Tiger Woods, St Andrews, 2000

270 (18 under-par), Nick Faldo, St Andrews, 1990; Tiger Woods, Royal Liverpool, 2006

Lowest Aggregates by Runner-Up

269 (68, 70, 65, 66), Jack Nicklaus, Turnberry, 1977; (69, 63, 70, 67), Nick Faldo, Royal St George's, 1993; (68, 66, 68, 67), Jesper Parnevik, Turnberry, 1994

Lowest Aggregates by an Amateur

281 (68, 72, 70, 71), Iain Pyman, Royal St George's, 1993; (75, 66, 70, 70), Tiger Woods, Royal Lytham, 1996

Lowest Individual Round

63, Mark Hayes, second round, Turnberry, 1977; Isao Aoki, third round, Muirfield, 1980; Greg Norman, second round, Turnberry, 1986; Paul Broadhurst, third round, St Andrews, 1990; Jodie Mudd, fourth round, Royal Birkdale, 1991; Nick Faldo, second round, and Payne Stewart, fourth round, Royal St George's, 1993

Paul Lawrie (1999)

Lowest Individual Round by an Amateur

66, Frank Stranahan, fourth round, Troon, 1950; Tiger Woods, second round, Royal Lytham, 1996; Justin Rose, second round, Royal Birkdale, 1998

Lowest First Round

64, Craig Stadler, Royal Birkdale, 1983; Christy O'Connor Jnr., Royal St George's, 1985; Rodger Davis, Muirfield, 1987; Raymond Floyd and Steve Pate, Muirfield, 1992; Miguel Angel Jimenez, Turnberry, 2009

Lowest Second Round

63, Mark Hayes, Turnberry, 1977; Greg Norman, Turnberry, 1986; Nick Faldo, Royal St George's, 1993

Lowest Third Round

63, Isao Aoki, Muirfield, 1980; Paul Broadhurst, St Andrews, 1990

Lowest Fourth Round

63, Jodie Mudd, Royal Birkdale, 1991; Payne Stewart, Royal St George's, 1993

Lowest First 36 Holes

130 (66, 64), Nick Faldo, Muirfield, 1992

Lowest Second 36 Holes

130 (65, 65), Tom Watson, Turnberry, 1977; (64, 66), Ian Baker-Finch, Royal Birkdale, 1991; (66, 64), Anders Forsbrand, Turnberry, 1994

Lowest Middle 36 Holes

130 (66, 64), Fuzzy Zoeller, Turnberry, 1994

Lowest First 54 Holes

198 (67, 67, 64), Tom Lehman, Royal Lytham, 1996
199 (67, 65, 67), Nick Faldo, St Andrews, 1990; (66, 64, 69), Nick Faldo, Muirfield, 1992

Lowest Final 54 Holes

199 (66, 67, 66), Nick Price, Turnberry, 1994

Lowest 9 Holes

28, Denis Durnian, first 9, Royal Birkdale, 1983
29, Peter Thomson and Tom Haliburton, first 9, Royal Lytham, 1958; Tony Jacklin, first 9, St Andrews, 1970; Bill Longmuir, first 9, Royal Lytham, 1979; David J. Russell, first 9, Royal Lytham, 1988; Ian Baker-Finch and Paul Broadhurst, first 9, St Andrews, 1990; Ian Baker-Finch, first 9, Royal Birkdale, 1991; Paul McGinley, first 9, Royal Lytham, 1996; Ernie Els, first 9, Muirfield, 2002; Sergio Garcia, first 9, Royal Liverpool, 2006

Successive Victories

4, Young Tom Morris, 1868-72 (no Championship in 1871).
3, Jamie Anderson, 1877-79; Bob Ferguson, 1880-82, Peter Thomson, 1954-56
2, Old Tom Morris, 1861-62; JH Taylor, 1894-95; Harry Vardon, 1898-99; James Braid, 1905-06; Bobby Jones, 1926-27; Walter Hagen, 1928-29; Bobby Locke, 1949-50; Arnold Palmer, 1961-62; Lee Trevino, 1971-72; Tom Watson, 1982-83; Tiger Woods, 2005-06; Padraig Harrington, 2007-08

Victories by Amateurs

3, Bobby Jones, 1926-27-30
2, Harold Hilton, 1892-97
1, John Ball, 1890
Roger Wethered lost a playoff in 1921

Champions in First Appearance

Willie Park, Prestwick, 1860; Tom Kidd, St Andrews, 1873; Mungo Park, Musselburgh, 1874; Harold Hilton, Muirfield, 1892; Jock Hutchison, St Andrews, 1921; Densmore Shute, St Andrews, 1933; Ben Hogan, Carnoustie, 1953; Tony Lema, St Andrews, 1964; Tom Watson, Carnoustie, 1975; Ben Curtis, Royal St George's, 2003

Justin Leonard (1997)   **Ben Curtis (2003)**

Padraig Harrington (2007, 2008)

Biggest Span Between First and Last Victories

19 years, JH Taylor, 1894-1913
18 years, Harry Vardon, 1896-1914
15 years, Gary Player, 1959-74
14 years, Willie Park Snr, 1860-75 (no competition 1871);
Henry Cotton, 1934-48

Biggest Span Between Victories

11 years, Henry Cotton, 1937-48

Champions in Three Decades

Harry Vardon, 1896, 1903, 1911
JH Taylor, 1894, 1900, 1913
Gary Player, 1959, 1968, 1974

Highest Number of Top-Five Finishes

16, JH Taylor, Jack Nicklaus
15, Harry Vardon, James Braid

Highest Number of Rounds Under Par

61, Jack Nicklaus
52, Nick Faldo
45, Tom Watson

Mark O'Meara (1998)

Highest Number of Aggregates Under Par

14, Jack Nicklaus, Nick Faldo

Most Consecutive Rounds Under 70

7, Ernie Els, 1993-94

Outright Leader After Every Round

Ted Ray, 1912; Bobby Jones, 1927; Gene Sarazen, 1932; Henry Cotton, 1934; Tom Weiskopf, 1973; Tiger Woods, 2005

Leader After Every Round Including Ties

Harry Vardon, 1899 and 1903; JH Taylor, 1900; Lee Trevino, 1971; Gary Player, 1974

Record Leads (Since 1892)

After 18 holes:
4 strokes, James Braid, 1908; Bobby Jones, 1927; Henry Cotton, 1934; Christy O'Connor Jnr., 1985
After 36 holes:
9 strokes, Henry Cotton, 1934
After 54 holes:
10 strokes, Henry Cotton, 1934
7 strokes, Tony Lema, 1964

Biggest Leads by Non-Champions

After 54 holes:
5 strokes, Macdonald Smith, 1925; Jean Van de Velde, 1999

Champions with Each Round Lower Than Previous One

Jack White, 1904, Royal St George's, (80, 75, 72, 69)
James Braid, 1906, Muirfield, (77, 76, 74, 73)
Henry Cotton, 1937, Carnoustie, (74, 73, 72, 71)
Ben Hogan, 1953, Carnoustie, (73, 71, 70, 68)
Gary Player, 1959, Muirfield, (75, 71, 70, 68)

Champion with Four Rounds the Same

Densmore Shute, 1933, St Andrews, (73, 73, 73, 73) (excluding the playoff)

Biggest Variation Between Rounds of a Champion

14 strokes, Henry Cotton, 1934, second round 65, fourth round 79
11 strokes, Jack White, 1904, first round 80, fourth round 69; Greg Norman, 1986, first round 74, second round 63, third round 74

Biggest Variation Between Two Rounds

20 strokes, RG French, 1938, second round 71, third round 91; Colin Montgomerie, 2002, second round 64, third round 84
19 strokes, RH Pemberton, 1938, second round 72, third round 91
18 strokes, A. Tingey Jnr., 1923, first round 94, second round 76
17 strokes, Jack Nicklaus, 1981, first round 83, second round 66; Ian Baker-Finch, 1986, first round 86, second round 69

David Duval (2001)

Best Comeback by Champions

After 18 holes:
Harry Vardon, 1896, 11 strokes behind the leader
After 36 holes:
George Duncan, 1920, 13 strokes behind the leader
After 54 holes:
Paul Lawrie, 1999, 10 strokes behind the leader

Champions with Four Rounds Under 70

Greg Norman, 1993, Royal St George's, (66, 68, 69, 64); Nick Price, 1994, Turnberry, (69, 66, 67, 66); Tiger Woods, 2000, St Andrews, (67, 66, 67, 69)
Of non-Champions:
Ernie Els, 1993, Royal St George's, (68, 69, 69, 68); Jesper Parnevik, 1994, Turnberry, (68, 66, 68, 67); Ernie Els, 2004, Royal Troon, (69, 69, 68, 68)

Best Finishing Round by a Champion

64, Greg Norman, Royal St George's, 1993
65, Tom Watson, Turnberry, 1977; Severiano Ballesteros, Royal Lytham, 1988; Justin Leonard, Royal Troon, 1997

Worst Round by a Champion Since 1939

78, Fred Daly, third round, Royal Liverpool, 1947
76, Paul Lawrie, third round, Carnoustie, 1999

Worst Finishing Round by a Champion Since 1939

75, Sam Snead, St Andrews, 1946

Best Opening Round by a Champion

66, Peter Thomson, Royal Lytham, 1958; Nick Faldo, Muirfield, 1992; Greg Norman, Royal St George's, 1993; Tiger Woods, St Andrews, 2005

Biggest Recovery in 18 Holes by a Champion

George Duncan, Deal, 1920, was 13 strokes behind the leader, Abe Mitchell, after 36 holes and level after 54

Most Appearances

46, Gary Player
38, Jack Nicklaus

Most Appearances on Final Day (Since 1892)

32, Jack Nicklaus
31, Alex Herd
30, JH Taylor
27, Harry Vardon, James Braid, Nick Faldo
26, Peter Thomson, Gary Player
23, Dai Rees
22, Henry Cotton

Most Appearances Before First Victory

16, Nick Price, 1994
14, Mark O'Meara, 1998

Most Appearances Without a Victory

29, Dai Rees
28, Sam Torrance
27, Neil Coles

Championship with Highest Number of Rounds Under 70

148, Turnberry, 1994

Championship Since 1946 with the Fewest Rounds Under 70

St Andrews, 1946; Royal Liverpool, 1947; Royal Portrush, 1951; Royal Liverpool, 1956; Carnoustie, 1968. All had only two rounds under 70.

Longest Course

Carnoustie, 2007, 7421 yards

Courses Most Often Used

St Andrews, 27; Prestwick, 24; Muirfield, 15; Royal St George's, 13; Royal Liverpool, 11; Royal Lytham, 10; Royal Birkdale, 9; Royal Troon, 8; Carnoustie, 7; Musselburgh, 6; Turnberry, 4; Deal, 2; Royal Portrush and Prince's, 1

Tom Lehman (1996)

Prize Money

Year	Total	First Prize
1860	nil	nil
1863	10	nil
1864	15	6
1876	27	10
1889	22	8
1891	30.50	10
1892	100	35
1893	100	30
1910	135	50
1920	225	75
1927	275	75
1930	400	100
1931	500	100
1946	1,000	150
1949	1,500	300
1953	2,500	500
1954	3,500	750
1955	3,750	1,000
1958	4,850	1,000
1959	5,000	1,000
1960	7,000	1,250
1961	8,500	1,400
1963	8,500	1,500
1965	10,000	1,750
1966	15,000	2,100
1968	20,000	3,000
1969	30,335	4,250
1970	40,000	5,250
1971	45,000	5,500
1972	50,000	5,500
1975	75,000	7,500
1977	100,000	10,000
1978	125,000	12,500
1979	155,000	15,000
1980	200,000	25,000
1982	250,000	32,000
1983	310,000	40,000
1984	445,000	50,000
1985	530,000	65,000
1986	634,000	70,000
1987	650,000	75,000
1988	700,000	80,000
1989	750,000	80,000
1990	825,000	85,000

Year	Total	First Prize
1991	900,000	90,000
1992	950,000	95,000
1993	1,000,000	100,000
1994	1,100,000	110,000
1995	1,250,000	125,000
1996	1,400,000	200,000
1997	1,586,300	250,000
1998	1,800,000	300,000

Year	Total	First Prize
1999	2,000,000	350,000
2000	2,750,000	500,000
2001	3,300,000	600,000
2002	3,800,000	700,000
2003	3,900,000	700,000
2004	4,000,000	720,000
2007	4,200,000	750,000

Attendance

Year	Total
1962	37,098
1963	24,585
1964	35,954
1965	32,927
1966	40,182
1967	29,880
1968	51,819
1969	46,001
1970	81,593
1971	70,076
1972	84,746
1973	78,810
1974	92,796
1975	85,258
1976	92,021
1977	87,615
1978	125,271

Year	Total
1979	134,501
1980	131,610
1981	111,987
1982	133,299
1983	142,892
1984	193,126
1985	141,619
1986	134,261
1987	139,189
1988	191,334
1989	160,639
1990	208,680
1991	189,435
1992	146,427
1993	141,000
1994	114,500

Year	Total
1995	180,000
1996	170,000
1997	176,000
1998	195,100
1999	157,000
2000	238,787
2001	178,000
2002	161,500
2003	183,000
2004	176,000
2005	223,000
2006	230,000
2007	154,000
2008	201,500
2009	123,000

The 138th Open Championship

Complete Scores

HOLE			1	2	3	4	5	6	7	8	9	10	11	12	13	14	15	16	17	18	
PAR	POSITION		4	4	4	3	4	3	5	4	4	4	3	4	4	4	3	4	5	4	TOTAL
Stewart Cink	T5	Round 1	4	4	4	2	4	2	5	3	4	3	4	4	3	4	3	4	4	5	66
USA	T9	Round 2	4	4	4	5	5	3	4	3	5	4	4	4	4	4	4	3	4	4	72
£750,000	T6	Round 3	4	4	4	3	5	3	6	4	4	4	2	4	4	4	4	4	4	4	71
		Round 4	4	4	4	3	5	3	4	4	4	5	2	4	3	5	2	5	5	3	69 **-278**
	1	Playoff					4	3											4	3	14
Tom Watson	T2	Round 1	3	4	3	3	4	3	5	4	4	3	3	3	4	4	3	4	4	4	65
USA	T1	Round 2	3	5	4	4	5	4	6	4	3	4	2	4	4	4	3	3	5	3	70
£450,000	1	Round 3	4	4	4	3	4	4	4	4	5	4	3	5	4	4	4	3	4	4	71
		Round 4	5	4	5	3	4	3	4	4	5	4	2	4	4	5	3	4	4	5	72 **-278**
	2	Playoff					5	3											7	5	20
Chris Wood	T51	Round 1	4	4	4	3	4	3	4	5	4	4	4	4	4	4	3	4	5	3	70
England	T22	Round 2	3	4	4	2	5	3	5	5	4	4	3	4	4	5	3	4	4	4	70
£255,000	T14	Round 3	4	5	4	3	4	4	4	4	4	5	3	3	4	4	4	5	4	4	72
	T3	Round 4	4	4	4	3	4	3	3	3	4	3	3	4	5	5	2	4	4	5	67 **-279**
Lee Westwood	T21	Round 1	3	3	3	3	4	3	6	4	4	4	3	3	4	4	2	6	5	4	68
England	T9	Round 2	4	4	4	3	4	3	5	5	4	4	3	4	4	4	2	5	4	4	70
£255,000	T4	Round 3	4	4	5	3	4	3	5	4	4	4	3	3	4	4	3	4	4	5	70
	T3	Round 4	4	4	4	3	5	2	3	4	4	5	3	4	4	4	4	5	4	5	71 **-279**
Luke Donald	T68	Round 1	4	4	5	3	5	3	4	4	5	4	3	4	4	3	3	3	5	4	71
England	T53	Round 2	3	4	5	3	6	4	4	5	3	4	3	4	4	5	3	4	4	4	72
£157,000	T27	Round 3	3	4	4	3	4	3	5	4	6	4	3	4	4	3	4	4	4	4	70
	T5	Round 4	3	4	4	2	4	3	5	5	4	3	3	4	4	5	2	4	4	4	67 **-280**
Retief Goosen	T10	Round 1	4	4	4	3	4	3	4	4	4	3	3	3	5	4	3	4	4	4	67
South Africa	T4	Round 2	3	4	4	3	5	3	5	4	5	4	4	4	3	4	3	3	5	4	70
£157,000	T4	Round 3	4	3	4	3	4	3	7	4	4	4	3	5	4	5	3	4	3	4	71
	T5	Round 4	4	5	4	3	4	3	5	4	4	4	3	4	4	5	4	4	3	4	72 **-280**
Mathew Goggin	T5	Round 1	5	3	4	2	4	3	4	3	4	4	3	4	5	4	3	4	4	3	66
Australia	T9	Round 2	4	4	4	4	4	3	5	5	5	4	3	4	4	4	3	4	4	4	72
£157,000	T2	Round 3	4	4	4	3	5	3	4	5	4	4	2	4	4	4	3	4	4	4	69
	T5	Round 4	4	5	4	4	4	3	4	4	4	3	3	4	4	5	4	5	5	4	73 **-280**

* Denotes amateurs

HOLE			1	2	3	4	5	6	7	8	9	10	11	12	13	14	15	16	17	18	
PAR	POSITION		4	4	4	3	4	3	5	4	4	4	3	4	4	4	3	4	5	4	TOTAL
Soren Hansen	T21	Round 1	4	4	4	2	4	2	4	4	4	3	3	4	3	4	3	6	5	5	68
Denmark	T22	Round 2	5	4	4	3	4	3	5	4	4	5	3	5	3	4	4	4	4	4	72
£90,400	T40	Round 3	5	4	4	4	5	3	5	6	4	3	3	4	4	5	3	4	4	4	74
	T8	Round 4	4	4	4	3	4	3	4	5	4	3	2	4	4	4	3	4	4	4	67 -**281**
Justin Leonard	T51	Round 1	4	4	4	3	4	3	4	4	6	4	3	5	3	4	2	5	3	5	70
USA	T22	Round 2	4	4	4	3	4	3	4	5	4	4	3	4	4	4	3	4	4	5	70
£90,400	T27	Round 3	4	4	4	3	5	3	5	4	4	3	4	4	4	4	4	5	4	5	73
	T8	Round 4	4	4	4	3	4	3	6	3	3	4	2	5	4	3	2	6	4	4	68 -**281**
Ernie Els	T37	Round 1	4	4	4	2	4	3	4	4	4	4	3	4	4	5	3	4	4	5	69
South Africa	T29	Round 2	5	4	4	3	4	4	4	5	5	4	3	4	4	4	3	4	4	4	72
£90,400	T27	Round 3	3	5	5	3	5	3	4	4	5	5	3	4	4	5	3	4	3	4	72
	T8	Round 4	3	4	4	3	4	3	4	4	4	3	3	5	3	4	3	5	4	5	68 -**281**
Thomas Aiken	T68	Round 1	5	5	4	3	5	3	4	4	4	4	3	4	6	3	4	3	3	3	71
South Africa	T53	Round 2	4	4	3	5	4	4	4	4	4	5	2	4	4	5	4	4	4	4	72
£90,400	T14	Round 3	3	4	4	3	4	3	5	4	4	3	3	4	5	5	3	4	4	4	69
	T8	Round 4	4	4	4	2	5	3	5	5	4	3	3	4	3	4	3	3	6	4	69 -**281**
Richard S Johnson	T51	Round 1	5	4	4	2	4	3	5	6	4	5	2	3	4	4	3	4	4	4	70
Sweden	T41	Round 2	3	4	5	3	4	3	7	4	5	5	3	4	4	4	2	3	4	5	72
£90,400	T10	Round 3	4	4	5	4	3	4	4	5	3	4	3	4	4	3	3	4	4	4	69
	T8	Round 4	4	4	6	3	4	2	4	5	3	3	3	4	4	6	2	5	4	4	70 -**281**
Jeff Overton	T51	Round 1	4	4	4	2	5	4	4	5	4	5	2	3	3	5	3	5	4	4	70
USA	T14	Round 2	4	4	3	3	4	4	4	5	5	5	3	4	4	3	2	4	4	4	69
£50,900	T43	Round 3	4	4	5	3	5	3	5	4	4	4	3	6	4	5	3	6	4	4	76
	T13	Round 4	3	4	5	3	4	3	4	4	4	4	3	4	4	4	2	4	4	4	67 -**282**
Andres Romero	T21	Round 1	4	5	3	3	3	3	4	3	4	4	3	5	6	3	4	4	4	3	68
Argentina	T41	Round 2	4	4	4	3	4	3	5	5	5	5	3	4	5	4	3	4	4	5	74
£50,900	T43	Round 3	5	5	5	3	4	3	3	4	4	3	3	4	4	4	5	6	4	3	73
	T13	Round 4	4	4	5	2	4	3	3	4	5	3	2	4	5	4	4	3	4	4	67 -**282**
Miguel A Jimenez	1	Round 1	4	3	4	3	4	2	4	4	3	4	3	4	4	4	3	4	4	3	64
Spain	T4	Round 2	4	5	5	4	4	4	5	3	5	5	3	3	4	4	3	4	4	4	73
£50,900	T27	Round 3	4	5	4	3	4	4	4	4	4	4	3	4	4	6	4	6	5	4	76
	T13	Round 4	4	3	4	3	5	3	4	4	4	4	4	3	4	5	2	3	6	4	69 -**282**
Matteo Manassero*	T68	Round 1	4	4	4	3	4	3	6	3	4	3	3	4	4	4	3	5	5	5	71
Italy	T42	Round 2	4	5	4	3	4	3	6	4	3	4	3	3	4	5	3	3	5	4	70
	T27	Round 3	4	4	4	3	4	3	5	5	3	4	4	5	4	4	3	4	5	4	72
	T13	Round 4	4	5	3	2	4	3	4	4	4	3	3	4	5	4	2	5	5	5	69 -**282**
Camilo Villegas	T5	Round 1	5	4	4	2	4	3	5	4	4	4	3	4	4	3	3	3	4	3	66
Colombia	T14	Round 2	4	4	4	3	5	3	5	5	4	5	3	4	3	5	3	4	4	5	73
£50,900	T14	Round 3	5	4	4	3	5	3	5	4	4	4	3	4	4	3	5	5	5	4	73
	T13	Round 4	4	4	4	3	6	3	4	5	4	3	3	4	3	4	3	5	4	4	70 -**282**
Justin Rose	T37	Round 1	4	6	4	3	5	3	4	4	3	4	4	3	4	4	3	3	4	4	69
England	T29	Round 2	4	4	4	3	4	3	5	5	5	4	3	4	5	4	3	4	3	5	72
£50,900	T14	Round 3	5	3	4	3	4	3	4	5	4	4	4	5	4	3	4	5	5	3	71
	T13	Round 4	4	4	5	3	4	4	4	4	3	4	3	4	4	4	4	4	4	4	70 -**282**
Francesco Molinari	T68	Round 1	3	4	4	3	4	3	4	3	4	4	3	3	4	4	4	6	7	4	71
Italy	T29	Round 2	4	4	4	3	4	3	5	5	4	3	2	4	4	4	3	6	4	4	70
£50,900	T14	Round 3	5	4	5	3	5	3	5	5	4	4	3	4	4	4	2	4	3	4	71
	T13	Round 4	3	4	4	3	5	4	4	5	4	4	3	4	4	4	3	4	4	4	70 -**282**

HOLE			1	2	3	4	5	6	7	8	9	10	11	12	13	14	15	16	17	18	
PAR	POSITION		4	4	4	3	4	3	5	4	4	4	3	4	4	4	3	4	5	4	TOTAL
Henrik Stenson	T68	Round 1	4	4	4	3	5	4	5	4	4	4	3	5	4	4	3	3	4	4	71
Sweden	T29	Round 2	4	4	4	3	5	3	4	4	5	4	3	4	4	4	2	4	5	4	70
£50,900	T14	Round 3	4	3	4	3	5	3	4	4	5	4	3	4	4	4	3	4	4	6	71
	T13	Round 4	4	4	4	3	4	4	4	4	4	4	3	5	4	5	2	4	4	4	70-**282**
Boo Weekley	T10	Round 1	4	3	4	3	4	3	4	4	5	4	3	4	4	4	3	3	4	4	67
USA	T14	Round 2	4	5	4	2	5	4	5	4	5	4	4	4	4	4	3	3	4	4	72
£50,900	T10	Round 3	4	4	4	3	4	4	6	3	5	4	2	4	5	4	3	4	4	5	72
	T13	Round 4	4	4	4	3	4	4	4	4	4	4	3	4	4	5	2	4	6	4	71-**282**
Thongchai Jaidee	T37	Round 1	3	4	4	3	5	4	4	4	4	4	3	4	3	4	3	4	4	5	69
Thailand	T29	Round 2	4	5	4	4	4	3	4	4	5	4	3	4	4	3	3	4	6	4	72
£50,900	T8	Round 3	4	4	4	3	3	3	4	4	3	5	3	4	4	5	3	5	4	4	69
	T13	Round 4	4	4	5	3	4	3	6	4	4	4	3	4	4	5	3	4	5	3	72-**282**
Ross Fisher	T37	Round 1	3	4	5	2	5	3	5	4	4	4	3	4	5	5	3	3	4	3	69
England	T4	Round 2	4	4	4	2	4	4	5	3	5	4	3	4	4	5	2	3	4	4	68
£50,900	T2	Round 3	4	4	3	3	5	3	5	4	4	4	3	5	4	5	3	3	4	4	70
	T13	Round 4	3	3	4	4	8	3	6	5	4	4	3	4	4	4	3	4	5	4	75-**282**
Peter Hanson	T51	Round 1	4	4	5	2	4	3	5	5	4	4	2	4	5	4	3	3	4	5	70
Sweden	T29	Round 2	4	4	4	3	4	3	5	6	5	4	3	3	4	5	2	4	5	3	71
£36,333	T27	Round 3	4	4	4	2	4	4	4	4	4	4	3	4	4	5	5	4	5	4	72
	T24	Round 4	5	5	4	3	4	3	5	4	4	4	3	4	4	4	2	4	5	3	70-**283**
Oliver Wilson	T98	Round 1	3	4	4	3	4	3	5	5	4	5	3	5	4	4	3	4	5	4	72
England	T41	Round 2	4	4	4	3	5	3	4	5	4	3	3	5	4	4	3	4	4	4	70
£36,333	T27	Round 3	4	4	4	3	3	2	5	5	5	3	5	3	5	4	5	4	4	4	71
	T24	Round 4	4	4	4	3	4	3	4	4	5	4	3	5	4	3	3	4	5	4	70-**283**
Angel Cabrera	T37	Round 1	3	4	4	3	5	3	4	4	4	4	3	6	3	4	3	4	4	4	69
Argentina	T14	Round 2	3	4	4	3	6	3	5	4	4	4	3	4	4	4	3	3	5	4	70
£36,333	T10	Round 3	4	5	4	3	5	3	5	5	4	4	3	4	5	4	3	4	4	3	72
	T24	Round 4	4	4	5	3	4	3	5	4	4	5	3	5	3	4	4	4	4	4	72-**283**
Davis Love III	T37	Round 1	4	4	4	2	5	4	5	5	4	4	3	3	4	3	3	4	5	3	69
USA	T41	Round 2	4	5	5	3	4	3	7	5	5	4	3	4	4	3	2	3	5	4	73
£29,357	T43	Round 3	5	4	4	3	5	3	5	4	4	4	2	4	5	4	3	4	5	5	73
	T27	Round 4	3	4	4	3	5	2	4	5	4	5	3	3	5	4	4	4	4	3	69-**284**
Soren Kjeldsen	T21	Round 1	4	4	4	3	3	3	5	4	4	3	3	4	3	3	4	6	4	4	68
Denmark	T65	Round 2	3	5	4	3	4	3	5	5	4	5	3	4	4	5	3	8	4	4	76
£29,357	T43	Round 3	4	4	4	3	5	2	4	4	4	4	3	5	4	4	4	4	5	4	71
	T27	Round 4	4	4	4	2	5	3	4	4	5	4	3	4	4	5	2	5	4	3	69-**284**
Nick Watney	T68	Round 1	5	5	4	3	4	3	4	4	5	4	3	4	4	4	3	4	4	4	71
USA	T53	Round 2	4	4	4	3	5	3	4	4	4	6	3	4	4	3	3	4	5	5	72
£29,357	T40	Round 3	4	4	4	3	5	2	6	4	4	4	3	4	3	4	5	4	4	4	71
	T27	Round 4	4	4	4	3	4	3	4	4	5	3	4	3	4	5	3	4	4	5	70-**284**
Mark Calcavecchia	T10	Round 1	4	3	5	3	4	3	4	4	4	4	2	4	4	4	3	4	4	4	67
USA	3	Round 2	4	5	4	3	5	3	4	4	4	3	3	3	4	3	4	4	5	4	69
£29,357	T27	Round 3	4	5	4	3	4	3	5	4	5	4	3	4	6	5	3	4	6	5	77
	T27	Round 4	5	4	4	2	5	4	4	4	3	4	3	4	4	4	4	4	5	4	71-**284**
Kenichi Kuboya	T2	Round 1	4	4	4	4	5	3	4	3	4	4	3	4	3	5	2	3	3	3	65
Japan	T4	Round 2	3	4	4	2	5	3	5	4	5	4	3	4	6	4	4	4	4	4	72
£29,357	T14	Round 3	4	4	4	3	4	3	5	5	6	3	3	5	4	5	3	4	6	4	75
	T27	Round 4	4	4	3	3	4	4	5	4	5	4	3	4	4	5	4	4	4	4	72-**284**

HOLE			1	2	3	4	5	6	7	8	9	10	11	12	13	14	15	16	17	18	
PAR	POSITION		4	4	4	3	4	3	5	4	4	4	3	4	4	4	3	4	5	4	TOTAL
James Kingston	T10	Round 1	4	5	4	3	4	2	3	3	5	4	4	4	4	3	4	4	3	4	67
South Africa	T9	Round 2	5	5	4	2	4	4	4	4	5	4	3	5	4	4	2	4	4	4	71
£29,357	T14	Round 3	4	4	4	3	5	4	5	4	5	5	3	5	4	4	3	4	5	3	74
	T27	Round 4	4	4	5	2	4	4	5	4	4	4	3	4	5	4	2	5	5	4	72 -**284**
John Daly	T21	Round 1	5	4	3	2	5	3	3	4	4	4	3	3	4	5	3	4	4	5	68
USA	T22	Round 2	4	3	4	3	4	3	5	5	6	4	3	4	4	5	3	4	4	4	72
£29,357	T14	Round 3	5	4	3	3	4	3	5	4	4	4	3	5	5	4	3	4	5	4	72
	T27	Round 4	4	4	6	3	4	3	4	6	4	4	3	4	4	4	3	5	3	4	72 -**284**
Richard Sterne	T10	Round 1	3	4	4	2	4	4	4	4	3	4	2	4	4	5	3	5	4	4	67
South Africa	T22	Round 2	4	4	4	4	4	3	4	4	5	4	3	4	5	4	4	3	4	6	73
£23,500	T43	Round 3	4	5	4	3	5	3	5	4	5	4	3	4	4	4	4	4	5	5	75
	T34	Round 4	3	4	4	2	4	3	4	4	4	4	3	5	4	4	5	4	4	5	70 -**285**
Martin Kaymer	T37	Round 1	4	5	4	3	4	3	5	4	4	3	3	4	4	5	3	3	5	3	69
Germany	T14	Round 2	4	4	5	3	4	3	6	5	4	4	3	3	3	4	3	4	4	4	70
£23,500	T27	Round 3	4	5	5	3	4	4	3	5	3	4	3	5	4	5	3	5	4	5	74
	T34	Round 4	4	4	4	3	4	4	4	4	4	4	3	5	4	3	4	4	6	4	72 -**285**
Graeme McDowell	T21	Round 1	3	4	3	3	3	4	5	5	3	4	3	4	4	4	2	6	4	4	68
Northern Ireland	T29	Round 2	4	4	4	3	4	3	7	4	5	4	3	4	4	4	4	4	4	4	73
£23,500	T14	Round 3	4	4	5	3	3	2	4	5	4	4	3	6	3	3	5	4	4	5	71
	T34	Round 4	4	5	4	3	4	3	4	6	5	4	3	3	5	4	4	3	4	5	73 -**285**
Jim Furyk	T10	Round 1	4	4	4	3	3	3	4	4	4	4	4	4	4	3	3	4	4	4	67
USA	T14	Round 2	4	4	4	3	6	4	5	4	4	4	3	4	4	4	3	4	5	4	72
£23,500	T6	Round 3	4	4	4	3	4	3	6	4	4	4	3	4	3	4	4	4	4	4	70
	T34	Round 4	4	5	5	3	4	3	5	5	4	5	4	4	5	4	4	4	4	4	76 -**285**
Sergio Garcia	T51	Round 1	4	4	4	3	4	3	3	4	5	4	3	4	4	4	2	6	4	5	70
Spain	T14	Round 2	3	4	4	4	4	3	4	4	5	4	4	4	4	4	2	4	4	4	69
£19,150	T43	Round 3	4	4	4	4	5	3	5	5	4	3	3	5	4	5	4	4	5	5	76
	T38	Round 4	4	5	3	3	4	3	4	5	3	6	3	3	5	4	3	4	5	4	71 -**286**
Thomas Levet	T68	Round 1	4	4	4	3	5	3	5	4	5	4	3	5	4	3	3	3	5	4	71
France	T65	Round 2	4	5	5	3	4	3	5	6	4	4	3	4	4	4	3	4	4	4	73
£19,150	T43	Round 3	6	4	4	3	5	3	4	4	3	3	3	3	4	5	4	4	4	4	71
	T38	Round 4	4	4	4	3	5	2	4	5	4	5	3	5	4	4	1	3	6	5	71 -**286**
Nick Dougherty	T51	Round 1	4	4	5	3	4	4	5	4	4	4	3	4	4	4	3	3	4	4	70
England	T22	Round 2	4	4	4	3	6	2	5	4	4	3	3	4	4	3	3	5	5	4	70
£19,150	T27	Round 3	4	5	5	4	4	3	5	4	4	5	3	3	4	4	4	4	4	4	73
	T38	Round 4	5	4	4	3	5	3	5	4	4	4	3	5	4	5	3	4	4	4	73 -**286**
Vijay Singh	T10	Round 1	4	4	3	3	4	3	5	3	4	4	3	4	3	4	3	4	5	4	67
Fiji	T4	Round 2	4	4	4	2	4	5	4	5	4	5	3	4	4	5	3	3	3	4	70
£19,150	T14	Round 3	5	5	4	3	5	2	5	5	4	4	3	4	4	4	4	5	4	5	75
	T38	Round 4	4	4	4	3	4	4	4	6	3	4	3	5	4	4	3	6	5	4	74 -**286**
Steve Marino	T10	Round 1	4	4	4	2	5	5	4	4	4	3	2	3	4	4	3	4	4	4	67
USA	T1	Round 2	4	5	3	4	3	2	6	4	4	5	3	4	4	3	3	4	3	4	68
£19,150	T10	Round 3	4	5	5	4	6	3	3	4	4	4	2	5	4	4	6	6	4	3	76
	T38	Round 4	5	4	5	3	3	4	4	5	4	5	3	5	4	4	3	5	4	5	75 -**286**
Anthony Wall	T21	Round 1	4	4	5	3	4	3	4	4	4	4	2	4	4	5	3	4	4	3	68
England	T22	Round 2	3	4	4	3	5	3	5	4	5	4	3	4	5	4	3	5	4	4	72
£15,688	T43	Round 3	5	4	5	4	3	4	5	4	4	5	3	4	5	5	2	4	5	4	75
	T43	Round 4	4	4	4	3	4	3	5	4	3	4	3	4	5	5	4	5	4	4	72 -**287**

HOLE			1	2	3	4	5	6	7	8	9	10	11	12	13	14	15	16	17	18	
PAR	POSITION		4	4	4	3	4	3	5	4	4	4	3	4	4	4	3	4	5	4	TOTAL
Branden Grace	T10	Round 1	3	4	4	4	4	3	4	4	5	4	3	4	4	4	2	4	3	4	67
South Africa	T14	Round 2	3	5	3	4	5	3	5	5	4	5	3	4	3	4	3	4	4	5	72
£15,688	T14	Round 3	4	5	4	3	3	4	5	5	4	3	4	4	4	5	3	5	4	4	73
	T43	Round 4	5	4	5	3	4	4	5	4	4	4	3	4	5	5	3	4	4	5	75 -**287**
Paul McGinley	T68	Round 1	4	4	5	3	3	3	5	4	4	4	3	4	4	5	3	4	5	4	71
Republic of Ireland	T41	Round 2	4	5	4	4	5	3	4	4	5	4	3	3	4	3	3	4	4	5	71
£15,688	T14	Round 3	4	3	4	3	5	3	4	4	4	4	3	5	4	4	4	4	4	4	70
	T43	Round 4	4	5	4	3	4	4	5	5	4	4	4	5	4	4	3	4	5	4	75 -**287**
Bryce Molder	T51	Round 1	4	5	4	3	4	3	5	3	5	4	3	3	4	5	3	4	5	3	70
USA	T53	Round 2	4	4	5	3	4	3	4	4	5	5	3	6	4	4	3	3	5	4	73
£15,688	T8	Round 3	4	4	5	3	5	3	5	3	3	4	3	3	4	4	2	4	4	4	67
	T43	Round 4	6	5	4	3	5	3	5	4	4	5	3	5	4	4	3	5	5	4	77 -**287**
Paul Lawrie	T68	Round 1	4	5	4	3	3	4	4	4	5	4	2	4	4	4	3	6	4	4	71
Scotland	T65	Round 2	4	4	4	3	4	3	6	4	6	5	3	4	3	5	3	4	4	4	73
£13,250	T68	Round 3	4	5	4	2	5	4	5	4	5	5	3	5	4	4	3	5	4	5	76
	T47	Round 4	4	4	3	3	4	3	2	4	4	4	3	7	4	5	2	4	5	3	68 -**288**
Zach Johnson	T51	Round 1	4	4	4	3	3	3	4	4	5	4	3	5	4	4	4	3	5	4	70
USA	T29	Round 2	4	4	4	3	5	3	6	4	5	3	3	4	3	4	3	4	5	4	71
£13,250	T59	Round 3	5	4	4	3	5	3	5	4	4	5	3	3	4	4	4	7	5	5	77
	T47	Round 4	4	4	4	3	4	3	4	4	4	4	3	4	5	5	3	4	4	4	70 -**288**
Paul Casey	T21	Round 1	3	4	3	3	3	4	3	4	4	4	3	5	4	5	3	4	5	4	68
England	T65	Round 2	4	4	4	4	6	4	4	6	5	5	3	4	4	4	3	4	4	4	76
£13,250	T59	Round 3	5	5	5	3	5	3	4	4	4	4	3	5	4	5	3	4	4	4	74
	T47	Round 4	4	4	4	4	4	3	5	4	4	4	3	3	3	4	3	4	6	4	70 -**288**
Rory McIlroy	T37	Round 1	4	3	4	3	4	3	4	6	3	5	3	4	3	5	3	3	5	4	69
Northern Ireland	T53	Round 2	3	5	4	4	6	3	5	5	4	5	3	4	3	5	3	4	4	4	74
£13,250	T56	Round 3	5	5	5	3	6	3	3	6	4	4	3	5	4	5	3	3	4	3	74
	T47	Round 4	4	5	4	3	4	4	4	6	4	3	3	4	4	4	3	4	4	4	71 -**288**
Gonzalo	T37	Round 1	3	4	4	3	4	4	4	4	5	4	3	4	5	3	3	4	4	4	69
Fernandez-Castano	T29	Round 2	4	4	4	2	5	3	4	5	5	5	3	4	4	4	3	5	4	4	72
Spain	T40	Round 3	4	5	4	3	4	3	6	4	4	3	4	6	5	3	4	4	4	3	73
£13,250	**T47**	Round 4	4	6	5	3	4	4	4	5	4	5	3	5	3	3	4	4	4	4	74 -**288**
Darren Clarke	T68	Round 1	4	4	5	3	4	3	4	4	4	6	3	5	4	3	3	4	4	4	71
Northern Ireland	T41	Round 2	4	5	4	2	5	2	4	4	5	5	3	5	4	4	3	4	4	4	71
£11,238	T68	Round 3	4	4	4	3	5	3	5	5	4	4	3	5	4	5	4	4	6	6	78
	T52	Round 4	3	4	4	3	4	3	4	4	4	3	3	4	4	5	4	4	5	4	69 -**289**
Kenny Perry	T68	Round 1	4	4	4	3	4	3	4	4	4	4	3	3	4	5	3	6	6	3	71
USA	T53	Round 2	3	4	4	3	4	3	5	5	5	4	3	6	3	4	3	4	5	4	72
£11,238	T59	Round 3	5	4	4	3	4	3	6	5	5	4	3	5	3	4	3	4	5	5	75
	T52	Round 4	4	3	5	2	5	4	4	3	3	5	3	4	4	4	3	4	6	5	71 -**289**
Graeme Storm	T98	Round 1	4	4	5	3	5	3	5	4	5	4	2	4	4	4	3	4	5	4	72
England	T65	Round 2	5	4	4	3	4	4	4	4	4	4	3	4	4	5	3	4	4	5	72
£11,238	T59	Round 3	4	4	4	3	6	3	5	5	4	4	3	5	3	6	4	4	3	4	74
	T52	Round 4	4	4	4	3	4	3	4	4	4	4	3	4	4	5	4	5	3	5	71 -**289**
Robert Allenby	T51	Round 1	4	4	4	2	4	3	5	4	4	4	3	4	5	4	4	4	5	3	70
Australia	T65	Round 2	4	5	4	4	4	3	4	4	5	5	3	5	3	4	3	4	5	5	74
£11,238	T56	Round 3	4	4	4	3	5	4	5	4	4	4	3	5	4	4	3	5	4	4	73
	T52	Round 4	4	4	4	3	5	3	5	5	4	3	2	4	4	4	4	4	5	5	72 -**289**

HOLE			1	2	3	4	5	6	7	8	9	10	11	12	13	14	15	16	17	18	
PAR	POSITION		4	4	4	3	4	3	5	4	4	4	3	4	4	4	3	4	5	4	TOTAL
Johan Edfors	T68	Round 1	4	4	4	2	5	3	5	4	4	5	2	4	4	4	3	6	4	4	71
Sweden	T65	Round 2	4	4	5	3	4	3	5	5	4	5	3	5	5	3	2	5	4	4	73
£11,238	T53	Round 3	4	5	4	2	4	4	4	4	5	4	3	5	4	5	3	5	4	3	72
	T52	Round 4	4	3	3	3	5	4	4	3	4	4	3	6	4	5	3	5	5	5	73 **-289**
Billy Mayfair	T37	Round 1	4	4	5	3	5	3	4	4	4	3	3	4	3	5	2	4	5	4	69
USA	T41	Round 2	4	4	5	3	5	3	5	4	5	5	3	4	4	3	4	4	4	4	73
£11,238	T43	Round 3	4	4	4	4	5	3	4	5	3	4	4	5	4	4	3	4	4	5	73
	T52	Round 4	4	5	4	3	5	3	5	5	4	5	3	4	4	5	3	4	4	4	74 **-289**
David Howell	T21	Round 1	4	4	4	2	4	2	4	4	3	4	3	4	4	4	5	4	6	3	68
England	T29	Round 2	4	4	4	3	5	3	5	5	5	3	3	4	4	5	3	5	4	4	73
£11,238	T27	Round 3	6	4	5	4	4	3	5	3	3	3	3	5	4	4	3	5	4	4	72
	T52	Round 4	4	5	4	3	5	3	4	4	5	4	3	4	5	5	5	5	4	4	76 **-289**
Steve Stricker	T5	Round 1	4	3	4	3	4	3	5	3	5	5	2	3	4	4	3	4	4	3	66
USA	T53	Round 2	4	4	4	2	5	3	6	5	4	5	4	3	5	5	3	5	5	5	77
£11,238	T27	Round 3	4	4	4	2	5	2	4	5	4	4	3	5	4	4	3	5	4	4	70
	T52	Round 4	4	4	4	3	4	3	5	4	4	4	2	5	5	4	4	6	5	6	76 **-289**
David Drysdale	T37	Round 1	3	4	4	2	4	3	6	4	4	3	4	4	4	4	3	5	4	4	69
Scotland	T41	Round 2	4	5	3	4	6	3	5	4	4	4	3	4	4	4	3	5	4	4	73
£10,450	T56	Round 3	4	4	5	5	5	3	4	4	4	4	3	4	4	4	3	6	5	4	75
	T60	Round 4	5	4	5	3	5	4	4	5	4	5	3	3	4	5	3	3	4	4	73 **-290**
Tom Lehman	T21	Round 1	4	4	4	3	4	3	4	5	4	4	2	4	3	4	3	3	5	5	68
USA	T41	Round 2	4	5	4	3	5	4	5	5	3	6	3	4	4	4	3	4	4	4	74
£10,450	T53	Round 3	4	4	5	3	5	3	5	4	4	4	3	5	4	5	3	4	5	4	74
	T60	Round 4	5	5	4	3	4	3	4	3	4	4	3	5	4	4	3	5	6	5	74 **-290**
Paul Broadhurst	T51	Round 1	4	4	5	4	4	3	4	4	4	4	3	4	3	4	3	4	5	4	70
England	T41	Round 2	4	4	3	3	5	3	5	4	4	4	3	4	5	5	4	4	4	4	72
£10,450	T53	Round 3	3	5	4	3	5	3	5	4	4	5	3	5	5	5	3	4	4	4	74
	T60	Round 4	5	3	4	3	4	3	7	5	4	4	3	5	4	5	2	4	5	4	74 **-290**
Kevin Sutherland	T37	Round 1	5	5	4	2	4	3	4	4	4	4	3	4	3	4	3	4	4	5	69
USA	T41	Round 2	4	5	4	4	4	3	5	5	4	4	3	4	5	4	3	4	4	4	73
£10,450	T43	Round 3	4	4	5	3	5	4	5	5	4	4	3	4	4	4	3	4	4	4	73
	T60	Round 4	4	4	4	3	2	4	4	3	4	4	3	5	4	9	4	4	5	5	75 **-290**
Ryuji Imada	T120	Round 1	4	4	4	3	3	4	6	5	4	4	3	5	4	5	3	4	5	4	74
Japan	T53	Round 2	4	5	4	3	5	3	6	3	4	4	3	4	3	3	3	4	3	4	69
£10,200	T72	Round 3	5	5	3	3	6	3	5	5	5	4	3	5	4	6	3	5	5	4	79
	64	Round 4	4	4	4	3	5	3	4	4	3	3	3	5	4	3	4	5	4	4	69 **-291**
Fredrik	T68	Round 1	4	5	5	2	3	4	4	4	4	4	3	5	4	4	3	4	4	5	71
Andersson Hed	T29	Round 2	3	5	3	2	5	3	5	4	4	5	3	4	4	4	3	4	4	5	70
Sweden	T64	Round 3	4	5	4	3	4	4	4	4	4	6	2	6	4	4	5	5	5	6	78
£9,950	**T65**	Round 4	3	4	4	3	4	3	5	4	4	4	3	4	7	3	3	4	5	6	73 **-292**
Padraig Harrington	T37	Round 1	4	4	4	3	3	3	5	4	4	4	3	4	4	4	3	5	4	4	69
Republic of Ireland	T53	Round 2	4	4	4	3	5	3	5	5	5	5	3	4	5	4	3	4	4	4	74
£9,950	T64	Round 3	3	4	5	3	4	3	6	6	4	4	3	5	4	5	3	5	5	4	76
	T65	Round 4	4	5	4	3	4	4	4	4	3	4	3	5	3	5	3	4	5	4	73 **-292**
Stuart Appleby	T68	Round 1	4	4	3	4	4	3	4	4	4	5	3	4	4	5	3	4	5	4	71
Australia	T53	Round 2	4	5	4	3	4	3	5	4	5	4	3	4	4	5	2	4	5	4	72
£9,950	T64	Round 3	4	4	5	4	4	4	5	5	3	4	4	4	5	5	4	4	4	4	76
	T65	Round 4	4	4	4	3	5	3	5	3	5	5	2	5	4	4	3	5	5	4	73 **-292**

HOLE			1	2	3	4	5	6	7	8	9	10	11	12	13	14	15	16	17	18	
PAR	POSITION		4	4	4	3	4	3	5	4	4	4	3	4	4	4	3	4	5	4	TOTAL
Sean O'Hair	T21	Round 1	3	4	5	3	3	3	7	3	4	4	2	4	5	4	2	4	4	4	68
USA	T53	Round 2	5	3	4	4	4	4	6	4	5	4	3	4	3	5	5	4	5	3	75
£9,950	T59	Round 3	5	4	4	3	5	3	7	4	4	4	3	4	4	4	4	5	4	4	75
	T65	Round 4	4	3	4	3	4	4	4	5	3	3	3	5	4	4	4	5	7	5	74 **-292**
JB Holmes	T21	Round 1	4	4	4	2	3	3	5	5	4	4	3	4	6	4	2	3	4	4	68
USA	T9	Round 2	4	4	4	2	5	3	4	5	5	4	3	4	4	4	2	5	4	4	70
£9,700	T27	Round 3	5	4	4	3	4	3	6	5	4	4	3	4	4	5	4	4	5	4	75
	69	Round 4	5	4	5	3	5	3	6	6	4	4	3	5	7	4	3	5	4	4	80 **-293**
Mark O'Meara	T10	Round 1	3	4	3	5	4	4	4	3	3	5	3	4	4	4	3	3	5	3	67
USA	T65	Round 2	5	4	4	5	5	4	5	5	4	4	3	5	4	4	3	4	4	5	77
£9,550	T70	Round 3	4	4	4	2	5	4	7	4	4	4	3	4	4	5	3	4	5	7	77
	T70	Round 4	4	4	6	3	5	3	5	4	4	4	2	5	4	4	4	4	5	4	74 **-295**
Fredrik Jacobson	T51	Round 1	4	3	4	2	4	3	4	4	4	4	2	4	4	3	7	5	5	4	70
Sweden	T41	Round 2	4	4	3	3	4	3	5	4	4	5	2	5	5	4	4	4	5	4	72
£9,550	T64	Round 3	4	4	5	4	3	6	3	6	3	4	7	3	5	5	4	3	4	4	77
	T70	Round 4	4	5	7	3	5	3	6	3	4	4	4	3	4	4	3	5	5	4	76 **-295**
Paul Goydos	T98	Round 1	3	5	4	4	5	3	4	5	4	4	3	3	4	6	3	4	4	4	72
USA	T65	Round 2	3	5	4	3	4	3	5	4	5	4	3	4	5	5	3	4	4	4	72
£9,400	T70	Round 3	5	4	5	4	5	5	5	4	4	4	3	5	4	4	3	6	4	3	77
	72	Round 4	5	5	5	3	5	3	6	4	4	5	4	4	5	5	3	7	4	5	82 **-303**
Daniel Gaunt	T140	Round 1	4	4	4	3	6	3	5	5	5	5	3	4	4	4	4	4	5	4	76
Australia	T53	Round 2	5	4	4	3	4	3	5	3	3	4	3	4	4	3	3	4	4	4	67
£9,300	T72	Round 3	4	4	4	3	6	4	5	4	3	5	3	6	4	5	4	7	4	4	79
	73	Round 4	5	4	3	3	6	4	5	4	4	4	4	4	6	5	4	8	5	4	82 **-304**

NON QUALIFIERS AFTER 36 HOLES

(Leading 10 professionals and ties receive £3,200 each, next 20 professionals and ties receive £2,650 each, next 20 professionals and ties receive £2,375 each, remainder of professionals receive £2,100 each.)

HOLE			1	2	3	4	5	6	7	8	9	10	11	12	13	14	15	16	17	18	
PAR	POSITION		4	4	4	3	4	3	5	4	4	4	3	4	4	4	3	4	5	4	TOTAL
Mike Weir	T10	Round 1	4	4	4	2	4	3	3	5	4	4	3	4	4	4	3	4	5	3	67
Canada	**T74**	Round 2	4	4	5	3	5	4	8	5	4	5	4	4	4	4	2	4	5	4	78 **-145**
Ben Curtis	T2	Round 1	4	4	4	4	3	3	3	4	4	5	3	4	3	3	3	3	4	4	65
USA	**T74**	Round 2	3	5	5	3	5	4	6	5	6	5	3	3	6	4	3	5	5	4	80 **-145**
Colin Montgomerie	T68	Round 1	4	4	4	3	4	3	4	4	4	4	4	4	5	5	3	4	5	3	71
Scotland	**T74**	Round 2	5	4	4	3	5	3	4	5	6	4	2	5	3	5	3	4	4	5	74 **-145**
Todd Hamilton	T131	Round 1	4	4	4	7	3	4	6	4	6	5	3	4	3	4	3	4	4	3	75
USA	**T74**	Round 2	3	4	4	3	4	3	5	5	5	4	3	5	4	4	2	4	4	4	70 **-145**
Charley Hoffman	T68	Round 1	4	4	4	4	6	3	4	4	4	4	3	4	4	4	3	4	4	4	71
USA	**T74**	Round 2	5	5	4	3	5	4	4	4	5	3	4	4	4	4	3	4	5	4	74 **-145**
Peter Hedblom	T68	Round 1	3	4	4	3	4	3	4	4	4	5	3	5	4	5	3	4	5	4	71
Sweden	**T74**	Round 2	4	5	5	3	3	4	5	4	5	4	3	4	5	4	4	4	4	4	74 **-145**
Josh Geary	T51	Round 1	4	4	5	2	5	3	5	4	4	4	3	4	4	5	3	3	4	4	70
New Zealand	**T74**	Round 2	4	5	4	3	5	3	5	5	5	5	3	3	5	4	3	4	4	5	75 **-145**

HOLE			1	2	3	4	5	6	7	8	9	10	11	12	13	14	15	16	17	18	
PAR	POSITION		4	4	3	4	3	5	4	4	3	4	3	4	4	4	3	4	5	4	TOTAL
Adam Scott	T68	Round 1	5	4	4	3	3	4	4	4	4	3	3	4	4	4	3	6	4	5	71
Australia	**T74**	Round 2	4	5	3	3	4	4	4	5	4	5	3	5	4	4	3	5	5	4	74 -145
Anders Hansen	T21	Round 1	4	4	4	2	3	3	5	5	4	4	2	5	4	4	3	4	5	3	68
Denmark	**T74**	Round 2	4	5	5	3	6	3	5	5	5	4	3	4	4	5	3	5	4	4	77 -145
Tiger Woods	T68	Round 1	4	3	5	3	4	3	4	4	4	5	2	4	4	4	4	5	5	4	71
USA	**T74**	Round 2	4	4	4	3	4	3	4	5	5	6	3	5	6	4	3	3	4	4	74 -145
DJ Trahan	T21	Round 1	4	4	4	2	4	4	4	4	4	4	3	4	3	4	4	4	4	4	68
USA	**T74**	Round 2	4	5	4	3	5	4	5	5	4	7	3	4	3	4	4	4	4	5	77 -145
Matt Kuchar	T51	Round 1	3	4	4	3	3	3	4	5	4	4	3	4	4	5	3	5	5	4	70
USA	**T85**	Round 2	4	5	4	3	5	3	5	4	5	5	3	4	5	4	3	5	5	4	76 -146
Tim Clark	T68	Round 1	4	4	4	4	4	4	3	4	6	4	3	4	4	3	3	4	5	4	71
South Africa	**T85**	Round 2	4	4	5	3	4	4	5	4	5	5	3	4	5	4	3	3	5	5	75 -146
KJ Choi	T120	Round 1	4	5	4	4	4	4	4	4	5	4	3	4	4	4	3	6	4	4	74
Korea	**T85**	Round 2	4	4	4	3	5	3	4	4	4	6	3	4	5	4	3	3	5	4	72 -146
Anthony Kim	T108	Round 1	4	9	4	3	3	3	4	4	4	3	3	4	4	4	3	6	5	3	73
USA	**T85**	Round 2	4	5	4	3	4	4	5	4	4	5	3	4	4	3	3	4	4	6	73 -146
Peter Baker	T120	Round 1	4	4	4	3	5	3	5	4	4	5	3	5	4	4	3	4	5	5	74
England	**T85**	Round 2	5	4	4	3	4	4	5	4	5	4	3	4	4	4	3	4	4	4	72 -146
Elliot Saltman	T51	Round 1	4	4	4	3	4	4	5	4	4	4	3	4	4	3	4	4	4	4	70
Scotland	**T85**	Round 2	5	4	5	3	5	3	5	5	4	4	2	5	3	6	4	4	4	5	76 -146
John Senden	T5	Round 1	4	4	4	3	4	3	5	4	4	4	3	4	3	3	2	4	4	4	66
Australia	**T85**	Round 2	5	5	5	4	5	3	5	5	5	5	3	4	4	4	5	4	4	5	80 -146
Louis Oosthuizen	T51	Round 1	4	4	5	3	5	3	5	4	3	4	3	4	3	4	2	4	6	4	70
South Africa	**T85**	Round 2	4	5	5	3	4	4	5	4	4	5	3	4	6	3	4	3	5	4	76 -146
Ryo Ishikawa	T21	Round 1	4	3	5	2	5	3	4	4	5	4	4	4	4	4	2	4	4	4	68
Japan	**T85**	Round 2	4	4	4	3	5	3	5	4	4	6	4	5	5	5	4	4	4	5	78 -146
Martin Laird	T120	Round 1	4	4	6	3	4	3	4	4	4	4	3	4	4	5	3	6	4	5	74
Scotland	**T85**	Round 2	3	4	4	3	4	4	5	6	4	4	4	4	3	4	3	4	4	5	72 -146
Ben Crane	T68	Round 1	4	4	5	3	4	3	4	4	5	5	3	4	3	5	3	3	4	5	71
USA	**T85**	Round 2	3	3	4	3	5	5	5	5	5	4	6	3	5	4	3	3	4	5	75 -146
Rhys Davies	T108	Round 1	4	4	4	4	5	4	4	4	5	4	3	4	4	4	3	4	4	4	73
Wales	**T96**	Round 2	3	5	4	3	4	4	6	4	5	4	3	4	4	5	4	4	4	4	74 -147
James Driscoll	T140	Round 1	4	5	5	3	4	4	5	4	4	4	3	4	5	4	3	5	5	5	76
USA	**T96**	Round 2	3	4	5	3	5	4	4	4	4	4	3	5	5	5	3	3	3	4	71 -147
David Toms	T98	Round 1	3	4	4	3	4	3	4	5	4	4	3	6	4	5	4	4	4	4	72
USA	**T96**	Round 2	4	4	4	3	4	3	5	5	4	4	3	4	5	4	5	4	6	4	75 -147
Rory Sabbatini	T120	Round 1	4	4	4	4	5	4	6	4	4	4	3	4	4	5	3	4	4	4	74
South Africa	**T96**	Round 2	5	4	4	3	5	4	4	4	4	4	3	4	5	4	4	4	4	4	73 -147
Charl Schwartzel	T68	Round 1	4	4	5	3	4	3	6	4	4	4	3	4	4	3	3	4	4	4	71
South Africa	**T96**	Round 2	5	3	4	3	5	4	5	6	4	5	3	4	5	4	3	4	4	5	76 -147
David Duval	T68	Round 1	5	4	5	3	4	4	4	4	4	4	2	6	4	4	3	3	5	3	71
USA	**T96**	Round 2	3	6	4	2	5	4	4	6	4	5	2	4	4	6	3	4	5	5	76 -147
Yuta Ikeda	T140	Round 1	5	5	4	3	4	2	4	6	5	4	3	5	4	4	3	7	4	4	76
Japan	**T96**	Round 2	5	4	4	3	4	2	4	4	4	3	4	4	4	5	3	4	5	5	71 -147
Richard Green	T68	Round 1	3	5	3	3	4	3	5	5	6	4	3	4	4	4	3	4	5	3	71
Australia	**T96**	Round 2	4	4	4	2	4	4	5	5	4	6	3	5	5	4	3	4	5	5	76 -147
Mark Brown	T68	Round 1	5	4	5	3	4	4	4	4	4	4	3	4	4	4	2	4	4	5	71
New Zealand	**T96**	Round 2	3	4	4	3	4	4	6	5	5	5	3	5	4	4	4	4	5	4	76 -147

HOLE			1	2	3	4	5	6	7	8	9	10	11	12	13	14	15	16	17	18	
PAR	POSITION		4	4	4	3	4	3	5	4	4	4	3	4	4	4	3	4	5	4	TOTAL
Briny Baird	T98	Round 1	3	4	5	3	5	4	5	4	4	5	2	4	5	4	3	5	4	3	72
USA	**T96**	Round 2	4	4	4	3	4	4	5	4	3	5	3	6	4	4	3	4	6	5	75 -147
Rod Pampling	T120	Round 1	4	4	4	3	5	3	5	4	4	5	3	5	4	4	3	6	4	4	74
Australia	**T96**	Round 2	3	4	5	3	4	3	5	5	5	4	3	4	4	5	3	4	5	4	73 -147
David Higgins	T108	Round 1	4	4	4	3	6	3	4	5	5	4	3	5	4	3	3	4	5	4	73
Republic of Ireland	**T107**	Round 2	3	4	4	3	5	3	5	5	5	6	3	5	4	6	2	4	4	4	75 -148
Gaganjeet Bhullar	T68	Round 1	4	7	5	2	5	3	4	3	3	5	3	4	4	6	2	3	4	4	71
India	**T107**	Round 2	4	3	4	3	6	3	6	5	4	4	3	4	6	5	3	4	5	5	77 -148
Sandy Lyle	T131	Round 1	4	6	6	3	5	2	5	4	4	3	3	4	4	5	3	3	6	4	75
Scotland	**T107**	Round 2	4	5	4	3	6	3	4	5	4	4	3	4	4	4	3	4	5	4	73 -148
Alvaro Quiros	T68	Round 1	4	4	4	3	4	3	4	4	4	3	3	6	4	4	3	4	5	5	71
Spain	**T107**	Round 2	5	5	5	3	5	3	4	5	5	4	3	6	4	6	3	3	4	4	77 -148
Charles Howell III	T108	Round 1	4	5	5	3	5	3	4	4	4	5	3	5	3	4	3	4	4	5	73
USA	**T107**	Round 2	4	4	5	3	5	3	4	3	4	7	3	4	4	3	3	3	8	4	75 -148
Gary Orr	T108	Round 1	4	4	4	3	4	3	6	5	4	4	3	4	4	4	3	4	5	5	73
Scotland	**T107**	Round 2	3	5	4	3	5	3	3	5	5	4	3	4	5	4	3	7	4	5	75 -148
Bubba Watson	T108	Round 1	4	4	4	3	5	3	4	5	5	5	3	4	3	4	2	4	6	5	73
USA	**T107**	Round 2	4	4	5	3	4	3	4	5	4	4	5	4	4	5	3	4	5	5	75 -148
Raphael Jacquelin	T131	Round 1	4	4	4	3	4	4	5	5	4	5	5	3	4	4	3	5	6	4	75
France	**T107**	Round 2	3	5	4	2	5	2	5	4	4	5	3	4	6	4	3	5	5	4	73 -148
Prayad Marksaeng	T108	Round 1	5	4	4	3	3	3	5	4	4	4	3	4	7	4	3	5	4	4	73
Thailand	**T107**	Round 2	7	5	4	3	4	3	5	4	4	5	3	4	4	5	3	4	4	4	75 -148
Markus Brier	T68	Round 1	4	4	4	4	4	3	4	5	4	6	3	4	4	3	3	4	4	4	71
Austria	**T107**	Round 2	5	4	4	2	4	4	6	4	5	5	3	4	5	4	3	6	5	4	77 -148
Robert Rock	T108	Round 1	4	4	4	3	4	3	5	4	4	4	4	5	5	4	3	4	5	4	73
England	**T107**	Round 2	3	4	4	3	5	5	5	5	3	4	2	6	5	4	4	4	4	5	75 -148
Brian Gay	T108	Round 1	4	4	5	6	5	3	4	3	4	5	3	4	4	4	3	4	4	4	73
USA	**T118**	Round 2	4	4	4	3	5	3	6	4	5	4	3	5	5	5	3	4	5	4	76 -149
Stephen Ames	T98	Round 1	5	4	3	3	5	4	4	4	4	4	3	6	4	4	3	4	4	4	72
Canada	**T118**	Round 2	4	4	5	3	4	3	6	6	4	5	4	5	4	4	3	4	4	5	77 -149
Lucas Glover	T98	Round 1	4	3	6	3	4	5	4	4	4	4	3	5	3	4	5	3	4	4	72
USA	**T118**	Round 2	3	5	3	3	6	4	5	3	5	6	3	5	6	4	2	4	5	5	77 -149
Stephan Gross*	T120	Round 1	4	4	4	3	5	3	4	4	6	4	3	5	4	6	2	4	5	4	74
Germany	**T118**	Round 2	5	4	4	3	5	3	5	5	5	4	3	3	4	5	3	4	5	5	75 -149
David Smail	T51	Round 1	4	4	4	3	4	3	4	4	4	6	3	5	3	5	3	3	4	4	70
New Zealand	**T118**	Round 2	4	5	5	3	5	3	5	5	4	5	3	6	6	5	3	4	4	4	79 -149
Rafa Echenique	T98	Round 1	4	5	4	3	4	3	4	5	3	4	3	5	3	5	4	4	5	3	72
Argentina	**T118**	Round 2	5	4	4	4	4	4	5	5	5	4	2	7	4	5	3	4	4	4	77 -149
Wen-chong Liang	T144	Round 1	4	4	4	3	4	4	5	5	5	5	3	5	3	6	3	5	5	4	77
China	**T118**	Round 2	4	5	4	3	5	3	5	4	5	3	3	4	5	4	3	4	4	4	72 -149
Azuma Yano	T131	Round 1	4	4	5	3	4	3	4	5	4	6	3	4	4	5	3	5	4	5	75
Japan	**T118**	Round 2	3	4	3	4	6	2	5	5	5	5	3	4	3	4	4	4	6	4	74 -149
Richie Ramsay	T144	Round 1	4	5	4	3	6	3	4	4	5	4	3	4	4	5	5	5	5	4	77
Scotland	**T118**	Round 2	4	4	4	3	6	2	4	5	3	5	3	5	4	4	3	4	4	5	72 -149
Brandt Snedeker	T98	Round 1	4	4	4	3	5	3	5	4	4	3	3	4	5	5	4	4	4	4	72
USA	**T118**	Round 2	4	5	4	3	5	5	4	4	5	4	4	5	5	4	2	4	5	5	77 -149
Tomohiro Kondo	T68	Round 1	4	4	4	3	4	3	4	4	4	3	4	5	4	4	3	4	5	5	71
Japan	**T128**	Round 2	3	5	4	3	5	4	5	5	5	6	4	4	4	5	4	5	3	5	79 -150

HOLE			1	2	3	4	5	6	7	8	9	10	11	12	13	14	15	16	17	18	
PAR	POSITION		4	4	4	3	4	3	5	4	4	4	3	4	4	4	3	4	5	4	TOTAL
Timothy Wood	T108	Round 1	4	5	4	4	4	4	3	5	5	4	3	4	6	4	3	4	3	4	73
Australia	**T128**	Round 2	5	4	4	3	4	3	5	5	5	6	3	4	5	5	3	6	4	3	77-150
Terry Pilkadaris	T21	Round 1	4	4	3	3	4	3	5	4	4	4	2	4	4	4	4	4	4	4	68
Australia	**T128**	Round 2	5	5	5	3	8	2	5	4	8	4	2	4	4	4	4	4	6	5	82-150
Steve Surrey	T37	Round 1	4	4	5	3	4	2	4	3	5	4	3	4	5	4	3	4	4	4	69
England	**T128**	Round 2	4	5	4	4	5	3	5	6	4	5	3	4	4	4	5	5	5	6	81-150
Chad Campbell	T108	Round 1	3	4	4	6	3	5	4	4	4	4	2	6	4	4	3	6	5	3	73
USA	**T128**	Round 2	4	4	4	3	4	5	5	4	6	4	3	4	5	4	3	4	7	4	77-150
Ken Duke	T68	Round 1	4	4	4	4	5	3	5	4	5	3	3	4	4	4	3	4	5	3	71
USA	**T128**	Round 2	4	4	5	3	5	4	5	5	5	6	3	5	5	4	3	4	5	4	79-150
Tim Stewart	T120	Round 1	4	5	5	3	5	3	3	5	4	3	3	5	4	5	4	4	5	4	74
Australia	**T134**	Round 2	3	4	4	2	5	4	5	5	5	6	3	5	5	4	3	4	4	6	77-151
Jeremy Kavanagh	T120	Round 1	3	4	4	3	4	2	4	4	4	5	3	5	3	5	3	6	7	5	74
England	**T134**	Round 2	5	4	4	3	5	3	5	5	5	7	3	3	4	6	3	4	4	4	77-151
Sir Nick Faldo	T149	Round 1	4	4	5	3	4	3	5	4	4	5	3	5	6	4	5	5	5	4	78
England	**T134**	Round 2	4	4	4	3	4	3	5	5	5	4	3	3	4	5	3	4	5	5	73-151
Hunter Mahan	T98	Round 1	5	5	4	3	4	3	6	4	4	4	3	4	3	4	5	4	4	3	72
USA	**T134**	Round 2	4	4	4	3	5	4	5	5	5	4	5	3	7	5	3	5	4	4	79-151
Carl Pettersson	T120	Round 1	4	4	4	3	4	3	4	6	4	4	2	7	4	5	3	5	4	4	74
Sweden	**T134**	Round 2	4	4	5	3	5	3	5	5	5	5	3	4	4	5	3	6	3	5	77-151
Richard Finch	T108	Round 1	4	4	4	3	4	3	4	4	5	4	3	4	4	4	4	5	5	5	73
England	**T134**	Round 2	4	6	4	5	5	5	4	4	5	5	3	3	4	4	3	4	5	5	78-151
Marc Cayeux	T131	Round 1	5	4	4	2	5	3	5	4	5	4	4	4	5	2	4	5	5	5	75
Zimbabwe	**T134**	Round 2	4	4	4	4	3	3	5	4	5	7	4	4	4	3	4	4	5	5	76-151
Damien McGrane	T149	Round 1	4	4	4	3	4	4	5	5	4	5	4	4	6	4	3	6	6	3	78
Republic of Ireland	**T141**	Round 2	4	5	3	3	5	3	5	4	5	5	3	4	4	5	3	4	4	5	74-152
Greg Norman	T144	Round 1	4	5	4	3	6	3	5	4	4	5	4	4	5	4	4	6	4	3	77
Australia	**T141**	Round 2	5	4	4	4	5	3	4	4	5	4	3	4	4	4	3	6	5	4	75-152
Lloyd Saltman	T131	Round 1	4	5	5	5	4	3	4	7	4	3	3	4	4	5	3	4	5	3	75
Scotland	**T141**	Round 2	5	3	4	3	6	3	4	5	5	6	3	4	3	5	3	5	4	6	77-152
Thomas Haylock	T120	Round 1	4	4	3	3	5	3	5	4	4	4	4	5	4	4	3	4	6	5	74
England	**T141**	Round 2	5	5	4	3	4	3	5	5	5	5	3	4	5	5	4	4	4	5	78-152
Geoff Ogilvy	T131	Round 1	3	4	4	2	4	5	5	6	3	4	3	4	5	5	4	5	5	4	75
Australia	**T145**	Round 2	4	4	4	5	5	3	6	6	4	5	3	4	4	4	3	4	5	5	78-153
Bruce Vaughan	T149	Round 1	4	4	4	3	4	4	5	4	4	5	3	4	4	6	3	6	5	6	78
USA	**T145**	Round 2	4	4	5	3	4	3	6	4	5	6	3	3	4	4	3	6	4	4	75-153
Ian Poulter	T131	Round 1	5	4	4	4	5	3	5	4	4	4	3	4	5	4	3	5	5	4	75
England	**T147**	Round 2	4	6	4	3	7	3	5	4	5	4	4	5	4	4	5	4	4	4	79-154
Koumei Oda	T140	Round 1	4	4	4	3	4	3	4	5	5	4	3	4	6	5	4	6	4	4	76
Japan	**T147**	Round 2	4	4	5	3	5	5	5	4	5	4	3	6	5	4	3	4	4	5	78-154
Dustin Johnson	T149	Round 1	5	4	4	3	5	3	4	5	5	8	2	4	4	4	3	4	4	7	78
USA	**T147**	Round 2	5	4	3	4	5	3	5	4	4	6	4	4	5	4	3	3	4	6	76-154
Daniel Wardrop	T131	Round 1	4	4	5	3	4	4	4	5	4	4	3	5	4	6	3	4	5	4	75
England	**150**	Round 2	4	4	5	3	4	3	6	4	5	4	4	5	4	6	3	6	5	5	80-155
Michael Wright	T144	Round 1	4	6	6	3	4	3	4	4	4	5	2	4	5	3	5	6	5	4	77
Australia	**151**	Round 2	4	5	4	2	5	3	6	4	4	3	5	4	4	5	5	6	4	6	79-156
Oliver Fisher	T154	Round 1	5	5	3	4	5	4	5	4	5	4	4	5	4	5	3	5	5	4	79
England	**152**	Round 2	4	5	4	4	5	3	5	4	4	5	3	6	4	4	4	5	4	5	78-157

HOLE			1	2	3	4	5	6	7	8	9	10	11	12	13	14	15	16	17	18	
PAR	POSITION		4	4	4	3	4	3	5	4	4	4	3	4	4	4	3	4	5	4	TOTAL
Pablo Larrazabal	T154	Round 1	4	4	5	4	5	3	4	4	4	5	3	6	5	4	5	4	4	6	79
Spain	**153**	Round 2	4	5	4	4	6	3	5	5	4	5	3	5	4	4	4	6	5	5	81 -**160**
Peter Ellebye	T144	Round 1	4	4	4	4	4	3	5	4	5	4	3	5	4	6	5	4	5	4	77
Denmark	**154**	Round 2	5	4	4	4	4	4	7	5	5	6	3	5	4	5	4	4	6	5	84 -**161**
Jaco Ahlers	156	Round 1	5	4	4	4	5	3	5	4	5	4	3	5	4	4	6	8	6	4	83
South Africa	**155**	Round 2	4	6	5	3	5	5	5	4	4	5	3	4	4	6	3	5	4	4	79 -**162**
Michael Campbell	T51	Round 1	4	5	7	3	3	3	5	5	4	4	4	4	4	4	3	6	6	4	78
New Zealand	**156**	Round 2	3	5	4	3	5	7	6	5	6	6	4	5							**WD**

Eagles/Birdies

1. Richard S Johnson 0/19
2. Steve Marino 2/16
3. Stewart Cink.................... 0/17
3. Graeme McDowell...........0/17
5. Jeff Overton.....................0/16
5. Tom Watson 0/16
7. Gonzalo Fdez-Castano 0/15
7. Ross Fisher....................0/15
7. Miguel Angel Jimenez.....0/15
7. Rory McIlroy...................1/14

Pars

1. Jim Furyk....................52
1. Retief Goosen 52
3. Angel Cabrera................51
3. Nick Dougherty 51
3. Henrik Stenson................51
6. Zach Johnson.................50
7. 8 players tied 49
59. Stewart Cink........................ 41

Bogeys

1. Paul Goydos 23
2. Branden Grace....................20
3. Stuart Appleby...................19
3. Johan Edfors 19
3. Gonzalo Fdez-Castano 19
6. James Kingston.................18
6. Billy Mayfair....................18
6. Sean O'Hair....................18
6. Steve Stricker 18
10. 5 players tied 17
41. Stewart Cink........................ 13

Double Bogeys/Worse

1. Michael Wright........... 7/0
1. Daniel Gaunt..............5/2
3. Chad Campbell................ 6/0
3. Lucas Glover 6/0
5. Michael Campbell 5/0
5. Pablo Larrazabal.............. 5/0
5. Graeme McDowell 5/0
5. Rory McIlroy 5/0
5. Geoff Ogilvy 5/0
5. Bruce Vaughan 5/0
5. Mark O'Meara 4/1
5. Fredrik Andersson Hed ... 4/1
5. Jaco Ahlers 3/2
103. Stewart Cink..................... 1/0

Driving Distance

1. Sergio Garcia 311.1
2. Nick Watney................. 308.9
3. Rory McIlroy............... 306.0
4. Branden Grace............. 303.6
5. Paul Casey 301.3
6. Angel Cabrera.............. 300.6
6. Daniel Gaunt 300.6
8. Vijay Singh.................... 299.9
9. Sean O'Hair.................. 299.5
10. Henrik Stenson............. 298.4
30. Stewart Cink.................... 291.9

Fairways Hit

Maximum of 56

1. Thongchai Jaidee..........42
2. Luke Donald.......................40
2. David Drysdale 40
4. Ernie Els 39
4. Ross Fisher 39
4. Zach Johnson 39
4. Francesco Molinari 39
4. Graeme Storm 39
4. Tom Watson 39
10. 6 players tied 38
33. Stewart Cink........................ 34

Greens in Regulation

Maximum of 72

1. Paul Casey 53
1. Thongchai Jaidee..........53
3. Angel Cabrera....................52
4. Ross Fisher.......................51
4. Davis Love III 51
4. Matteo Manassero............51
4. Lee Westwood...................51
8. 6 players tied 50
23. Stewart Cink........................ 47

Putts

1. Soren Kjeldsen............110
2. David Howell.....................112
3. Fredrik Jacobsen..............115
3. Miguel Angel Jimenez......115
3. Jeff Overton......................115
3. Richard Sterne 115
7. Steve Marino 116
7. Camilo Villegas.................116
9. Stewart Cink...................... 117
9. Martin Kaymer.................117

Statistical Rankings

Courtesy of Unisys

	Driving Distance	Rank	Fairways Hit	Rank	Greens In Regulation	Rank	Putts	Rank
Thomas Aiken	293.0	24	31	52	50	8	122	32
Robert Allenby	291.6	33	33	38	44	48	127	66
Fredrik Andersson Hed	286.3	51	31	52	45	37	122	32
Stuart Appleby	288.9	42	29	60	43	53	121	26
Paul Broadhurst	285.4	53	33	38	48	17	129	72
Angel Cabrera	300.6	6	29	60	52	3	128	70
Mark Calcavecchia	293.8	20	36	21	45	37	120	19
Paul Casey	301.3	5	37	16	53	1	132	73
Stewart Cink	291.9	30	34	33	47	23	117	9
Darren Clarke	297.9	11	37	16	44	48	120	19
John Daly	280.1	62	32	42	47	23	125	58
Luke Donald	279.3	64	40	2	50	8	121	26
Nick Dougherty	282.5	56	33	38	45	37	124	51
David Drysdale	289.4	40	40	2	44	48	124	51
Johan Edfors	288.1	43	29	60	46	29	126	64
Ernie Els	275.0	69	39	4	48	17	124	51
G Fernandez-Castano	286.6	49	36	21	45	37	125	58
Ross Fisher	282.5	56	39	4	51	4	124	51
Jim Furyk	287.4	48	34	33	47	23	122	32
Sergio Garcia	311.1	1	32	42	46	29	122	32
Daniel Gaunt	300.6	6	25	70	36	70	123	39
Mathew Goggin	288.0	47	34	33	48	17	123	39
Retief Goosen	292.4	27	35	26	47	23	120	19
Paul Goydos	285.8	52	32	42	33	73	125	58
Branden Grace	303.6	4	25	70	46	29	124	51
Soren Hansen	291.8	31	35	26	50	8	124	51
Peter Hanson	280.3	61	27	65	45	37	120	19
Padraig Harrington	271.6	72	32	42	36	70	119	14
JB Holmes	297.3	14	32	42	40	63	123	39
David Howell	290.6	37	32	42	37	69	112	2
Ryuji Imada	284.3	54	33	38	43	53	119	14
Fredrik Jacobson	289.4	40	26	68	36	70	115	3
Thongchai Jaidee	295.6	17	42	1	53	1	128	70
Miguel Angel Jimenez	276.5	68	32	42	42	56	115	3
Richard S Johnson	276.8	67	37	16	48	17	119	14
Zach Johnson	290.0	39	39	4	47	23	123	39
Martin Kaymer	277.1	66	31	52	39	67	117	9
James Kingston	271.0	73	29	60	40	63	119	14
Soren Kjeldsen	288.1	43	36	21	42	56	110	1
Kenichi Kuboya	293.3	22	35	26	45	37	118	11
Paul Lawrie	293.3	22	23	73	41	60	118	11
Tom Lehman	277.4	65	31	52	42	56	125	58
Justin Leonard	297.9	11	37	16	48	17	118	11
Thomas Levet	282.5	56	38	10	49	14	123	39
Davis Love III	294.5	19	32	42	51	4	124	51
Matteo Manassero*	291.3	35	31	52	51	4	125	58
Steve Marino	297.6	13	27	65	40	63	116	7
Billy Mayfair	290.8	36	38	10	46	29	127	66
Graeme McDowell	293.0	24	38	10	46	29	123	39
Paul McGinley	288.1	43	35	26	44	48	121	26
Rory McIlroy	306.0	3	27	65	44	48	121	26
Bryce Molder	275.0	69	31	52	45	37	121	26
Francesco Molinari	283.5	55	39	4	46	29	120	19
Sean O'Hair	299.5	9	26	68	40	63	120	19
Mark O'Meara	274.4	71	31	52	41	60	123	39
Jeff Overton	280.4	60	25	70	41	60	115	3
Kenny Perry	293.6	21	37	16	45	37	123	39
Andres Romero	296.4	16	34	33	46	29	119	14
Justin Rose	291.4	34	32	42	50	8	127	66
Vijay Singh	299.9	8	36	21	46	29	123	39
Henrik Stenson	298.4	10	32	42	47	23	122	32
Richard Sterne	292.1	28	35	26	38	68	115	3
Graeme Storm	292.6	26	39	4	45	37	127	66
Steve Stricker	286.5	50	34	33	45	37	123	39
Kevin Sutherland	279.5	63	28	64	45	37	122	32
Camilo Villegas	288.1	43	31	52	43	53	116	7
Anthony Wall	281.3	59	35	26	42	56	123	39
Nick Watney	308.9	2	35	26	50	8	126	64
Tom Watson	295.0	18	39	4	48	17	121	26
Boo Weekley	296.6	15	38	10	49	14	123	39
Lee Westwood	291.8	31	38	10	51	4	120	19
Oliver Wilson	292.0	29	36	21	49	14	125	58
Chris Wood	290.1	38	38	10	50	8	122	32

NON QUALIFIERS AFTER 36 HOLES

	Driving Distance	Rank	Fairways Hit	Rank	Greens In Regulation	Rank	Putts	Rank
Jaco Ahlers	284.0	105	10	152	19	132	68	149
Stephen Ames	285.0	99	16	72	20	114	61	46
Briny Baird	288.0	84	17	60	21	98	63	88
Peter Baker	297.8	35	19	29	20	114	62	67
Gaganjeet Bhullar	290.3	63	12	135	20	114	61	46
Markus Brier	298.8	32	16	72	18	140	59	20
Mark Brown	289.5	67	17	60	20	114	65	126
Chad Campbell	309.5	5	18	42	21	98	61	46
Marc Cayeux	292.5	53	14	116	23	53	69	151
KJ Choi	286.0	92	15	94	19	132	59	20
Tim Clark	280.3	124	21	9	25	27	65	126
Ben Crane	293.8	47	15	94	22	74	62	67
Ben Curtis	284.3	104	18	42	22	74	63	88
Rhys Davies	288.3	79	18	42	22	74	66	138
James Driscoll	283.5	109	12	135	17	147	62	67
Ken Duke	291.0	60	13	128	22	74	67	144
David Duval	297.8	35	12	135	23	53	64	109
Rafa Echenique	289.0	73	18	42	22	74	64	109
Peter Ellebye	280.0	126	12	135	16	150	70	154
Sir Nick Faldo	288.3	79	14	116	21	98	66	138
Richard Finch	294.8	45	16	72	20	114	63	88
Oliver Fisher	266.5	149	14	116	14	154	63	88
Brian Gay	266.3	150	15	94	20	114	63	88
Josh Geary	275.5	139	11	143	20	114	62	67
Lucas Glover	297.8	35	16	72	22	74	59	20
Richard Green	288.5	78	15	94	20	114	60	31
Stephan Gross*	302.8	14	15	94	20	114	64	109
Todd Hamilton	289.3	70	19	29	23	53	60	31
Anders Hansen	267.8	148	14	116	22	74	62	67
Thomas Haylock	281.0	120	17	60	19	132	66	138
Peter Hedblom	287.0	88	18	42	25	27	66	138
David Higgins	279.8	127	13	128	22	74	61	46
Charley Hoffman	307.5	7	15	94	27	8	68	149
Charles Howell III	288.3	79	11	143	22	74	60	31
Yuta Ikeda	299.3	28	12	135	19	132	57	5
Ryo Ishikawa	305.3	10	11	143	23	53	63	88
Raphael Jacquelin	293.8	47	19	29	25	27	69	151
Dustin Johnson	314.0	2	16	72	21	98	65	126
Jeremy Kavanagh	256.3	155	10	152	21	98	63	88
Anthony Kim	311.3	4	17	60	24	42	61	46
Tomohiro Kondo	280.8	121	15	94	19	132	65	126
Matt Kuchar	301.8	16	20	16	23	53	65	126
Martin Laird	283.8	107	18	42	25	27	66	138
Pablo Larrazabal	283.0	111	10	152	14	154	65	126
Wen-chong Liang	279.5	129	17	60	20	114	64	109
Sandy Lyle	276.0	138	13	128	20	114	60	31
Hunter Mahan	299.8	24	16	72	18	140	60	31
Prayad Marksaeng	288.3	79	16	72	26	20	64	109
Damien McGrane	283.5	109	17	60	20	114	63	88
Colin Montgomerie	290.3	63	19	29	21	98	62	67
Greg Norman	274.5	141	14	116	21	98	64	109
Koumei Oda	285.8	94	11	143	16	150	62	67
Geoff Ogilvy	279.8	127	15	94	19	132	61	46
Louis Oosthuizen	284.8	102	16	72	22	74	63	88
Gary Orr	278.5	131	13	128	19	132	61	46
Rod Pampling	262.3	152	14	116	22	74	64	109
Carl Pettersson	285.3	98	12	135	18	140	63	88
Terry Pilkadaris	291.3	58	20	16	23	53	64	109
Ian Poulter	259.3	153	16	72	16	150	58	12
Alvaro Quiros	304.3	13	11	143	25	27	67	144
Richie Ramsay	282.5	113	18	42	20	114	61	46
Robert Rock	289.0	73	13	128	24	42	67	144
Rory Sabbatini	285.0	99	16	72	25	27	70	154
Elliot Saltman	281.3	116	15	94	25	27	69	151
Lloyd Saltman	288.8	75	15	94	21	98	64	109
Charl Schwartzel	272.0	144	11	143	18	140	57	5
Adam Scott	298.5	33	16	72	23	53	63	88
John Senden	278.0	135	16	72	24	42	64	109
David Smail	286.0	92	19	29	22	74	62	67
Brandt Snedeker	278.3	133	16	72	22	74	63	88
Tim Stewart	284.5	103	11	143	18	140	61	46
Steve Surry	299.5	26	14	116	21	98	64	109
David Toms	288.0	84	20	16	21	98	62	67
DJ Trahan	270.5	146	21	9	20	114	60	31
Bruce Vaughan	278.5	131	14	116	22	74	64	109
Daniel Wardrop	270.3	147	8	155	16	150	61	46
Bubba Watson	289.5	67	12	135	20	114	63	88
Mike Weir	284.0	105	20	16	27	8	67	144
Timothy Wood	282.0	115	17	60	18	140	61	46
Tiger Woods	286.8	89	15	94	21	98	58	12
Michael Wright	285.8	94	12	135	17	147	63	88
Azuma Yano	288.8	75	11	143	17	147	62	67

TURNBERRY

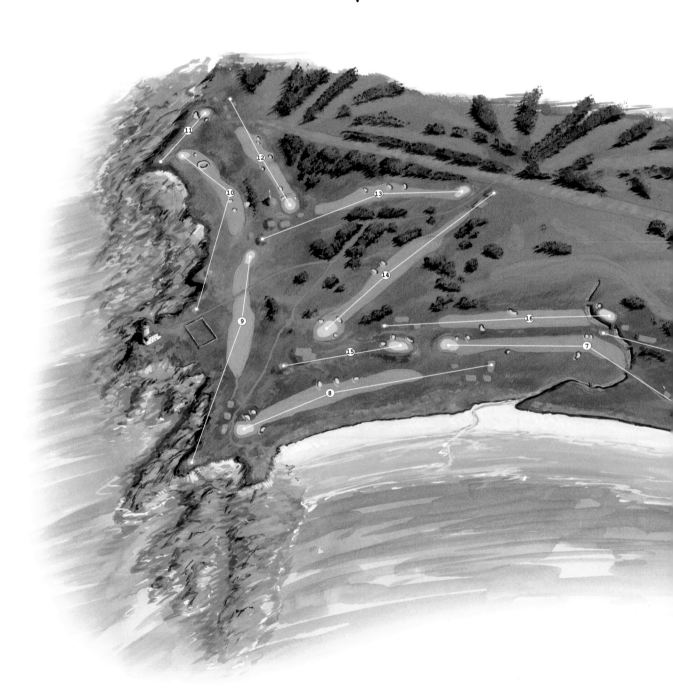